STUDENT-FRIENDLY GUIDES

# Perfect presentations!

PETER LEVIN & GRAHAM TOPPING

Open University Press

Open University Press
McGraw-Hill Education
McGraw-Hill House
Shoppenhangers Road
Maidenhead
Berkshire
England
SL6 2QL

email: enquiries@openup.co.uk
world wide web: www.openup.co.uk

and Two Penn Plaza, New York, NY 10121-2289, USA

First published 2006

A catalogue record of this book is available from the British Library.

ISBN–10: 0 335 21905 5 (pb)
ISBN–13: 978 0335 21905 6 (pb)

Library of Congress Cataloging-in-Publication Data
CIP data applied for

Typeset by YHT Ltd, London
Printed in the UK by Bell & Bain Ltd, Glasgow

# Contents

## Part One: Finding your voice

## Part Two: Preliminaries

## Part Three: Preparing your materials

## Part Four: Thinking about your audience

# List of Exercises

# List of Tables

# Speaking to an audience with confidence and clarity

# READ THIS FIRST!

For most people, the prospect of having to speak to an audience, if it's not something they do very often, is an intimidating one. If you're a student who has to give a presentation in a class, seminar or tutorial, and you get 'nerves' beforehand, or if you would simply like to be a more effective presenter, this book will help you to develop the communication skills and confidence you need.

Skills and confidence in public speaking will last you all your life. They will stand you in good stead in other situations besides academic ones. Whether you're giving a presentation at work, giving an account of yourself at an interview, making a speech at a wedding or speaking up at a public meeting, they will help you to say what you want, clearly and persuasively.

One definition of 'university' could well be 'a place where they expect you to do things that they don't actually teach you'. Thus it is the norm for your teachers to expect you to give a presentation without it entering their minds that they should take the trouble to teach you how to do it. Fortunately it *is* possible for you – indeed for anyone – to learn these skills. The learning process involved is not an academic, book-driven one. Rather, it is what's known as 'experiential learning'.

Experiential learning is both a cyclical process and a progressive one. (Like a corkscrew, it goes round and round and at the same time moves forward.) The cycle has three stages: you have experiences (such as that of speaking to an audience); you reflect on those experiences and see what can be learned from them; then you work out ways of doing things differently – better – next time. You then start round the cycle again, and go on to gain further experiences by trying out these different ways next time around.

The progressive part of 'experiential learning' is a progression from doing things consciously to doing them unconsciously – doing them without

**1**

having to think about what you're doing. When you're learning a new skill – driving a car, running a new computer program, playing a sport – you start off being very conscious of what you're doing. The chances are you'll be consulting manuals, rule books and textbooks, being told things, putting questions to your instructors: you're getting a lot of stuff into your head. As you gain experience, however, you do this less and less. You 'internalize' your learning, so that doing the right thing becomes second nature to you. It's like developing a habit: a behaviour goes into your conscious mind, then into your unconscious mind, then out of your conscious mind. In this book we aim to help you to develop good habits in giving presentations.

You can do a lot to develop your own good habits by observing other people's presentations, both good and bad. Observing bad presentations will help you to avoid getting into some bad habits. Whether in lectures or in presentations by your fellow students, have you ever experienced any of the following?

- You can't follow the speaker's reasoning.
- You can't tell which are the important points you need to take away with you.
- The speaker loses his or her way, gets flustered, and you get embarrassed too.
- There's so much material on the slides that you can't get it all down (and sometimes the speaker keeps talking while you're trying to do so, which makes matters worse).
- The presentation doesn't seem to address the prescribed topic or to answer the question set.
- The speaker treats you to a lot of assertions but doesn't back them up with evidence.
- You're bored: you stop paying attention and your mind wanders to other things.
- The speaker reads his or her script or notes and avoids eye contact with you or any other member of the audience.
- The speaker speaks quietly and/or mumbles, so you find it difficult to hear and make out what is being said.
- The speaker seems not to care about the material or getting a message over to the audience.

Simply noticing these experiences gives you a head start in working out ways of avoiding them for yourself. Clearly you need to pay attention to four interrelated things:

1. The material – the content, the subject matter – that you're presenting. Knowing your stuff, and knowing you know it, gives you confidence and helps to give your audience confidence in you.
2. The organization (structure) of your presentation. It must be organized in such a way that it holds your audience's attention and they find it easy to follow you.
3. Your relationship with your audience. A speaker who can quickly establish rapport with his or her audience has a head start when it comes to giving a successful presentation.
4. How you are feeling. You don't just need confidence in your material. If – like just about everybody else – you suffer from 'nerves' before you give a presentation, you need to tame these so that they help rather than hinder you when the time comes.

In this book we deal with all of these. You will find practical exercises that will help you to develop yourself as a speaker, together with suggestions and recommendations to help you when you actually have a presentation to give.

Communication skills are essentially 'soft' in nature. Everyone's skills have to be moulded to their personality. Some presentation trainers ignore this. They lay down 'hard' rules: *Do* this! *Don't* do that! Some training offers rules that seem to capture common sense, but actually don't mean much: for example, 'Speak loudly and slowly!' But how loud is loud enough? How slowly can you speak before your audience goes to sleep?

We believe that any rules you follow have to be flexible, and congruent with your experience, your understanding and your personal feelings and preferences. There is no single 'one size fits all' approach. There are many ways in which you can relate to an audience. We aim to help you to be aware of these, and to choose the ones you're most comfortable with and that you find most effective, so you can develop your own personal toolkit of skills and techniques. If you understand how the tools work, and how to gauge their effect, you will use the ones that are right for the subject matter, right for your audience and right for you.

*Peter Levin & Graham Topping*

# Introduction

## The idea of 'presentation'

By **presentation** we mean a talk or speech given by a **presenter** (sometimes more than one) to an **audience** of two or more people. A successful presentation is not only given *to* the audience, it is given *for* the audience. It certainly isn't just a speech launched in the general direction of the audience with a 'take it or leave it' attitude. It follows that when you are preparing a presentation you should always have the needs and interests of your audience at the forefront of your mind. Your presentation is for them.

Please note that we think in terms of giving a presentation, not delivering it. We regard a presentation as a kind of gift from presenter to audience, not something that is dumped in front of them, like milk left on a doorstep.

Every audience is made up of individuals, and each has its own particular make-up: a particular mix of men and women, of people from different age groups, possibly of people from different countries. Different audiences may have different proportions of people with a good knowledge of the subject of your presentation, of native and non-native speakers of English, of people who share your sense of humour. Unless an audience comprises a group that meets regularly, it is unlikely to have exactly the same make-up as any other that you have met and to react to you in exactly the same way. It's important to be aware of this. You are asking for trouble if you treat an audience as if it is a standard or homogeneous group. Successful presenters take the trouble to ensure that there is 'something for everyone' in their presentations.

This book is about spoken presentations rather than 'performance' presentations, such as a piece of theatre, a recitation of poetry, music, song or dance. However, all such performances share something with spoken presentations: they take place in real time and in a space that is shared between the 'performer' and the audience. So it is not surprising that some principles apply to such performances as well as to spoken presentations. Spoken presentations are commonly augmented by **visual aids** (or '**visuals**'), such as slides projected on to a screen using an overhead projector (OHP), computerized slides displayed using a program such as PowerPoint, or film clips. A whiteboard and/or flipchart may also be used to present material visually. The presentation may be augmented by **handouts**, documents containing text or pictures or both, which are given to the audience before or after the presentation and which they are able to take away with them.

As you no doubt know, there are many different kinds of presentation. There is the *academic presentation*, as given in a classroom, lecture theatre or conference hall. There's the *sales pitch*, which you use when you have a product you want to sell. There's the *job interview*, when in effect you are selling yourself. There's the *formal report*, as made by the officers of an organization to its annual general meeting or to a committee meeting. Then there's the *after-dinner speech*, when the speaker is usually expected to entertain the audience.

Whatever the kind of presentation, there is always a **topic**, a subject, which you may be able to choose for yourself or which may be assigned to you in the form of a **brief** for your presentation: 'This is what I/we want you to do.' (The person – or people – who has drawn up your brief may well be sitting in the audience.) And there is always a **setting** – the environment, both physical and organizational – within which your presentation takes place.

Every presentation constitutes a **communication** between presenter and audience. The presenter invariably has a **message** that he or she wishes to communicate to their audience. We can think of such communication as the presenter performing a **handover** to the audience, almost as if the message were something physical. A successfully communicated message often incorporates one or more **soundbites**, pithy and memorable expressions.

However, the audience members at a presentation gain more than their perceptions of the presenter's message: they gain an **impression** of the presenter himself or herself. At a job interview in particular, this will be crucial. It will matter to the interviewers not only what answers you give to their questions but, for example, whether you give the impression of being someone who will fit into their organization.

## The ingredients of a successful presentation

Presenters who are consistently successful usually have **goals** and **objectives** clear in their minds. We find it useful to think of a 'goal' as something that we want to *achieve*, to bring about, and an 'objective' as something that we want to *do* – an action that we want to take – in order to achieve our goal. Thus the relationship between goals and objectives is a relationship between ends and means.

One of your goals when you're preparing a presentation might be that the audience should go away afterwards having grasped five points and understood their significance, and your objective – your means to that end – might be to spell out and illustrate each of those five points as clearly as you can.

During a presentation messages are given in other ways besides the presenter's speech and showing of visual aids. When you're giving a presentation, the audience will observe, consciously or unconsciously, your **body language** – your movements and postures – and will notice whether or not you establish **eye contact** with them. They will draw conclusions about your attitudes and feelings from their experience of both your body language and eye contact.

When a presentation is taking place there will always be some kind of relationship between presenter and audience. In a good presentation there will usually be a **rapport** between presenter and audience, and an **energy** that the presenter and audience will share. This energy may take many forms, from shared good humour, even laughter, to the kind of silence and focus in which you could hear the proverbial pin drop. We can think of this energy as filling the space between presenter and audience.

A presenter will always possess certain attributes. Besides physical attributes, such as height and the ability to speak clearly, **commitment** – to serving your audience, and to getting your message across – can be crucial to the success of a presentation. If you are psychologically committed to these objectives – if you positively identify yourself with them – you will find yourself putting more energy into the event than if you are not.

A successful presenter will not only possess useful attributes: he or she will have learned to deploy useful general **skills** and particular **techniques**. (We use the word 'skills' to refer to strategy, 'techniques' to refer to tactics. Thus a useful skill is that of getting your message to stick in the minds of your audience; a useful technique for achieving that objective is that of making the same point in different ways.)

A presenter should be **authentic** and also **congruent** with the message and setting, and with his or her audience: they have to match each other, to be all of a piece. Take that well-known form of presentation, the lecture. When the presenter is someone who has a reputation in the field, when the message is an authoritative one ('I have done the research, and this is what I have found'), when the physical setting is a one-facing-many auditorium and when the organizational setting is one where the presenter talks from a position of authority (lecturer, professor or honoured guest), then (a) the presenter is being authentic, and (b) presenter, message and setting are congruent.

Every presentation is made up of **material**: content, subject matter, information, know-how, argument, conclusions, a 'message'. In a good presentation the material will be logically organized, structured: it will have a clear plan designed to enable the audience to follow it. The plan of a presentation plan serves as an agenda or 'route map'; in the presenter's mind it might be a list of headings, a diagram or a picture, for example. As a presenter, you will usually find it well worthwhile first getting your plan clear in your own mind, then sharing it with your audience. Then both you and they can refer to it at any point to see where you have got to and where you are heading.

## Presentations versus writings

In an academic context, it is worthwhile noting the similarities and differences between presentations and writings, such as essays, reports and articles. One similarity is that both presentations and writings are usually addressing a specific topic. Another is that both need to have a logical structure that the reader or audience can follow. So if the brief is in the form of a question, say, both a presentation and an essay on it will have a structure that leads logically from the question to the answer to it. (For more on structuring essays, see *Write great essays!* in the same series as this book.)

However, there are important differences between presentations and writings that you must be aware of. Compare the situation of watching and listening to somebody else's presentation with that of reading an article, say. You have two very different experiences. With a presentation, the pace – the speed – of the presentation is set by the presenter, not by you sitting in the audience. You can't take time out to disentangle a complicated sentence or to re-read and digest a paragraph, as you can when reading an article. You can't flip to the end to see what the conclusions will be, whether in fact an answer will be given to the question posed, for example. It can be much less easy to tell where you are in the proceedings if the presenter doesn't provide an agenda or 'route map'. It follows that when *you* are the presenter you have to make allowances for your audience's situation. We make suggestions for doing this in the section entitled 'Make your presentation audience-friendly' (pages 87–88). Above all, do avoid the trap of thinking that all a presentation requires is that you write an essay and then read it out to your audience.

## The structure of this book

This book is divided into eight parts, as you can see from the Contents pages. Each part is divided into a number of sections. Part One – 'Finding your voice' – is designed to familiarize you with what we see as the elements of speaking to an audience: breathing and relaxing; creating energy; using body language and eye contact; and conquering your nerves. The remaining parts are all designed to help you when you are actually faced with having to give a presentation. Part Two – 'Preliminaries' – deals with things that you need to know and do before you can get started. Part Three – 'Preparing your materials' – will help you work on your message and the visual aids and handouts you need, as well as the prompts (script, index cards, notes or annotated printouts) that you want to use. Part Four – 'Thinking about your audience' – will remind you that your presentation has to be tailored to your audience's needs and characteristics, and will help you if you find yourself struck by nerves.

Part Five – 'Rehearse! Rehearse! Rehearse!' – offers you ideas about what to do in the run-up to your presentation, to ensure that it goes smoothly on the day. Part Six – 'Last-minute checks' – will help you to ensure you won't be taken by surprise by the room you'll be working in and the equipment you'll be using. Part Seven – 'Giving your presentation' – is designed to help you to use your skills to good effect and to deal capably with any question-and-answer sessions. Part Eight – 'Evaluation' – will help you to take a cool look at how your presentation went and to draw useful lessons for next time.

# Part One

# Finding your voice

# Training your body

Most people are endowed by nature with more 'vocal power' than they think. If you feel you have a 'small voice' it is because you have learned – probably unconsciously, especially if it's a cultural trait – to physically obstruct your voice by constricting your chest cavity and the airways between your mouth and your lungs. Such constriction can also come about because you are physically tense; indeed, anxiety about giving a presentation can give rise to the tension that produces that 'small voice' effect.

All of us also carry voice-obstructing physical tensions in our bodies a lot of the time. For example, many people go around with their shoulder muscles tense, and this has the effect of damping down the potentially powerful vocal resonances they can create in their upper chests.

It follows that if you want to develop your ability as a speaker, you need to start by training your body to free up your voice. In this section we offer some exercises that will help you to do this.

# Relaxing

There are many simple relaxation techniques – it's simply a question of finding those that work for you. You may know some already. There are many sources on the web: type 'relaxation techniques' into a search engine and you will find plenty. You need to try them out for yourself. Here we suggest two exercises that you will find in most guides to relaxation techniques.

**Exercise 1: Deep breathing**

*Purpose*
This is an exercise to slow your heart rate and breathing, and relax some of the muscles associated with breathing.

*Equipment*
A private, quiet room.

*What you do*
This exercise is best done standing up but, if you have to, you can sit. First, count aloud from one to five (take about five seconds for this) and then do the same thing in reverse (i.e. count aloud from five down to one). Do this two or three times to establish a rhythm. Now carry on counting silently, in your head, and as you do so breathe in slowly – filling your lungs with air – over that slow count from one to five, then breathe out again slowly as you count down from five to one. Try to get comfortably empty by one.

Do this as many times as you can, up to ten times. As you become more accustomed to doing it, try to extend the count progressively to seven and then to ten.

### Exercise 2: Tensing and releasing

*Purpose*
This is an exercise to reduce the tension in your muscles. It can be applied to just about every muscle in your body.

*Equipment*
A private, quiet room.

*What you do*
This exercise works by *increasing* the tension in the muscle(s) and then suddenly releasing it. Say you want to work on your hands and arms: curl your fingers into the palms of your hands and tighten them into a fist. (You can do this standing or sitting.) Gradually – over a few seconds – extend the tension to your wrists, then your forearms and eventually your biceps, until your arms are as taut and rigid as your fist. Two or three more seconds and you'll feel like you want to explode. Now suddenly release the tension: let your arms flop and shake your hands vigorously away from you (your arms will move too, of course), as if there's chewing gum stuck to your fingers and you want to shake it off. Repeat this exercise a couple of times if you feel like it.

You can tense your facial muscles too (try 'collapsing' your face into a tight ball around your mouth, hold for a few seconds, then shake gently until your jaw and cheeks wobble), and those in your shoulders and chest (cross your arms and hunch down almost into a foetal position), in your feet, calves and thighs (just as you did with your hands and arms), or indeed in any part of your body.

## Voice preparation

Your voice is a physical instrument. Training your voice is rather like sports training. Actors work on their voice daily, like an athlete in training. Exercise 3 will have a progressive building-up effect over a period of weeks, but you will start seeing results immediately, which can be very useful if you have a presentation to give very soon.

### Exercise 3: Freeing up your voice

*Purpose*
This is a set of exercises to relax the muscles that surround your voice-producing mechanism. It addresses five sets of muscles – neck, jaw and tongue, throat, shoulders, and spine – and also incorporates breathing and articulation exercises.

*Equipment*
A private, quiet room.

*What you do*
To start, stand with your feet apart, and with your weight equally distributed between left and right feet, and between the heels and balls of your feet. If you find it difficult to locate that balance, rocking backwards and forwards and from side to side may help you locate it. Now, consciously extend your spine in a straight column, so that your head is high, and your ribcage comes up. For followers of Alexander technique, it's as though your body is suspended from a point at the top of your skull. Students can think of this position as the exact opposite of the academic 'slump' or 'slouch'.

*Neck*
This exercise works by using the weight of your head to stretch your neck muscles. Do *not* use your muscles to 'push' or 'pull' your head down.

1. *Nodding.* Keeping your spine erect, drop your head forward on to your chest as if a heavy weight down by your feet in front of you is hanging by a thread from your nose or chin. Hold this 'nodding' position for a moment. Now imagine gently raising that weight so that your head comes back to the upright position and then drops back, so you're looking up towards the ceiling and your jaw is flopping open. The weight is now hanging down behind your heels. Hold this 'looking up' position for a moment. Now raise your head slowly to the upright and then resume the 'nodding' position, letting the weight of your head do the work. Repeat this two or three times.

2. *Earwigging.* Looking in front of you, and keeping your spine erect and shoulders level, let your head drop sideways, to the left, so your left ear moves towards your left shoulder as far as it can go. Then repeat the action on your right-hand side, moving your right ear towards your right shoulder. Repeat this two or three times.

3. *Head rotating.* Start by looking in front of you, with your spine erect and shoulders level. Now, without moving your shoulders, turn your head to the left, until you feel your right neck muscles gently stretching. Then turn your head to the right and stretch your left neck muscles. Repeat this two or three times.

*Jaw and tongue*
This looks strange, so do it in private!

Chew an imaginary piece of gum. It starts pea-sized and you chase it around your mouth with your tongue. As you chew, it magically gets larger, until after half a minute it fills your mouth so that your jaws are forced as wide as possible. As you reach this peak of tension around your mouth, immediately stop chewing, relax and shake your head from side to side so your lower jaw wobbles independently of your upper one.

*Throat*
This exercise opens the throat passage, allowing sound to emerge freely. Try the steps separately, then join them together one after another.

1. Start with your head down on your chest. Breathe in slowly and very deeply, raising your head until you're looking at a spot just ahead of you on the ceiling. Your head is now tilted well back and your whole thorax is full of air.

2. Breathe all the way out, making the sound 'Haaaaa' as if you are trying to warm the spot on the ceiling with your breath.

3. Still looking at the spot on the ceiling, breathe sharply back in again, while making the sound 'Ka'. (It will probably take you a few practice attempts before you find this easy to do!)

4. Now let the air out of your lungs slowly, letting your head drop slowly on to your chest.

Repeat the sequence of steps several times. The hard 'Ka' sound in step 3 is essential.

*Shoulders*
In many people, their shoulders carry tension, and this considerably affects their voice.

Raise both your arms to 90 degrees to the side of your body, so your arms and body form a 'T'. Keeping your arms outstretched, start moving them from your shoulders with a circular motion, so that you draw two circles with your fingertips. Start with a circle the size of (the diameter of) a table-tennis ball, then a CD, then a football, and on towards a circle the size of a lorry wheel. Then work your way back down to the table-tennis ball. Finally, let your arms flop, relax your elbows, and shake your hands and arms vigorously from the shoulder as if to dislodge chewing gum that's stuck to your fingers.

If you haven't much space, you can do a version of this exercise making circles with your shoulders – big shrugs! – while keeping your hands down by your sides.

*Spine*
This is another exercise you might not want other people to see! It's a way of releasing tension from the muscles in the lower back by making exaggerated S-shaped movements in the spine.

First make the S-shape from side to side, throwing your hips out first to the left then to the right. Then make the S-shape from front to back, which involves alternately thrusting your pelvis forwards, then back, while moving your chest in the opposite direction. Do both of these moves several times. The front-to-back one is definitely one to keep to yourself – or for someone who knows you very well!

*Breathing*
Breathe in on a slow (silent) count of ten, and then breathe out again over a count of ten. Repeat this. Then repeat it again – the third breath – and this time make a humming 'Mmmm' sound *immediately* you start breathing out, and continue making this sound for the count of ten. Picture in your mind's

eye the vibration of that sound in your mouth, and try to move it forward until it makes your (loose) lips vibrate. Actors call this 'placing your voice forward', and it gives a life and vigour to your voice. It gets easier with repetition. After a while, instead of the 'Mmmm', use a phrase that you might use in a presentation, and try to feel the vibration at your lips.

*Articulation*

Many people with big voices swallow the ends of their words, or slur their speech, running one word into the next. Words need to be articulated separately, so they are distinct to the listener. Fortunately, to correct swallowing or slurring requires only the following simple physical exercises.

1. Take a deep breath, then make consonant sounds in rapid succession, like a machine gun. Maybe 'd-d-d-d-d-d-d-d', repeated three times; then 'm-m-m-m-m-m-m-m', again repeated three times; then 'k-k-k-k-k-k-k', similarly repeated, and so on. (Four groups of eight of each consonant seems to work well, but you can be flexible about this.) When your breath runs out, take a good lungful of air and carry on.

2. Have a stock of three or four 'tongue twisters'. Examples are 'Round the rugged rocks the ragged rascal ran' and 'Peter Piper picked a peck of pickled pepper. Here's the peck of pickled pepper Peter Piper picked.' You may know others, perhaps in other languages. Take a deep breath and say them aloud. As you practise them, try to increase your speaking speed, and to speak more forcefully and distinctly. If you do this properly, you will find your mouth and lips making big movements in an effort to articulate sounds precisely. It's a workout for your mouth muscles!

You won't want to make these strange shapes in front of any audience, but the exercises tone up your everyday, flaccid muscles so they can make more precise sounds.

# Using body language and eye contact

## Developing good habits

Because of the ease with which body language and eye contact patterns can be misread, it is crucial for the purposes of presentation that you develop good habits. The good news is that you don't have to consciously control all your body movements – indeed, such control is almost impossible to achieve without years of physical training. What you *can* do is to take a leaf out of the book of actors and try some of the very simple skills they use to make their body language and use of eye contact help their performance.

Actors think in terms of 'objectives', and commit themselves to achieving those objectives. An objective exists in their heads, but the commitment to achieving it – the sense of importance and urgency – brings about appropriate body language and eye contact.

Here's an example. If your objective was 'to get across a crowded room without being noticed by person X', you would of course register where that person was standing and in which direction he or she was facing. More importantly, you would move in a particular way. You would hold your head at an angle, you would place your feet carefully and softly, make only small movements with your arms, avoid making eye contact with X, and so on, doing all this entirely instinctively, not as a result of your brain sending conscious instructions to your body. If your objective was rather different, 'to cross the room so that X definitely notices you', you would still register X's position, but your head would be up, your feet would stride out, your arms would probably make quite big movements, and you would be looking in X's direction; again, you would be doing this instinctively.

This example holds an important lesson for you. When you're giving a presentation, you must have firmly in your mind this objective: to communicate *this* message *now* to *that* person in the audience. (And then another idea, perhaps to another person, and so on.) If you are strongly committed to communicating your message, this will show – automatically! – in your body language and use of eye contact. You can try this out in Exercises 4 and 5, below. These exercises are also good practice for finding the right level of commitment when giving a presentation.

It's important not to be distracted from your objective. If a 'rogue' objective invades your mind – 'I must get to the bank before it closes', say – your audience will notice this and will conclude, correctly, that you are not 100 per cent committed to your task of communicating your message to your audience. They, in their turn, are likely to be distracted.

**Exercise 4: Using body language and eye contact (part one)**

*Purpose*
This is an exercise to help you appreciate how your commitment to communicating your message changes almost every aspect of your body language and eye contact, and how those change in the listener too.

*Equipment*
Two friends of yours and a private, quiet place with three chairs.

*Material*

*Either* part of a presentation you have already prepared in script or note form *or* day-to-day material such as the rules of a game that you're familiar with. Don't tell your friends beforehand what material you're going to use. Have a pen and paper handy (for the friend who will be the 'observer').

*Set-up*

You are going to be the 'speaker'. Ask one of your friends to be your listener. This person, the 'listener', has no further instruction: his or her task is to do nothing more than listen to you!

Ask your other friend, who will be the 'observer', to notice the body language and eye movements of both you and the listener. The observer should jot down notes on the posture of both you and the listener, the angle at which each of you is holding your head, gestures that you make, where your eyes are looking, your facial expression, and anything else that he or she notices.

*What you do*

First, imagine yourself (the speaker) in the following situation. You and the listener are both stuck on a train station. You've been there for hours already, there is no sign of your train and you're resigned to waiting at least another hour. You've run out of things to say. Then you suddenly remember you have something else you can talk about: your material (your part-presentation or the rules of the game that you know).

Now you open your mouth and speak to the listener using your material. You're going to speak for about one minute. You are speaking just to pass the time, not because you really care about the subject, nor because you think the listener is interested. It's just to pass the time. Speak for roughly one minute, then stop. (The listener doesn't say anything; the observer is also silent but makes very brief notes.)

Once your minute is up, stand up, give your arms and legs a little shake, then sit down again in the same chair. Imagine a new situation. You're in a train station again, waiting for a long-delayed train. Again you find something to say. (You're going to use exactly the same material.) But this time your message is *important*! If the listener does not understand every single sentence you utter, then something terrible will happen. Maybe a bomb will go off and people will be hurt; maybe a mutual friend will miss out on a fortune. It's *crucial*, a matter of life or death, that your listener understands what you're saying. Use the same material – don't change the content. Once again, speak to the listener for about one minute, while the listener listens in silence and the observer observes and jots down notes.

Once your minute is up, again, stand up, give your arms and legs a little shake, then sit down again in the same chair. Ask the observer to say what differences he or she saw in your body language and that of the listener and in the pattern of eye contact between you.

We would expect the observer to report considerable differences in body language and eye contact between the two 'runs'. Perhaps you as the speaker leaned forward more in the second case, faced the listener more directly, made gestures with your hands, widened your eyes and raised your eyebrows more and/or held eye contact for more of the time. No doubt the listener's body language changed too.

There should be three lessons for you here. First, you already have a repertoire – a vocabulary, as it were – of body language and eye movement; you can use this in giving presentations and you can develop it. Second, the exercise shows you how your level of commitment to conveying your message both influences and is revealed by your body and your eyes. Third, although the listener will have been affected by your way of speaking – emphasis, loudness, and so on – as well as your use of your body and eyes, the exercise will almost certainly show you how the combination – body, eyes and way of speaking – can have a powerful effect on your audience.

When you have played your role as speaker, your friends can take their turn. You will learn something from being a listener and an observer as well as from being a speaker.

### Exercise 5: Using body language and eye contact (part two)

This is a refined version of Exercise 4, but you should do that exercise first.

*Purpose*
This is an exercise to help you to use your body language and eye contact in a more sensitive way. The equipment, material and set-up are the same as in Exercise 4.

*What you do*
First, close your eyes and imagine that you are speaking in a 'normal' conversational tone, as if you were recounting your material over lunch, with no time pressure. Then open your eyes and get ready to speak for real.

For your first run, slightly *lower* your level of commitment to recounting your material. Imagine that you are putting a little less energy into it; it's less urgent that you get your message over. Talk for about a minute. As in Exercise 4, the listener silently listens and the observer observes and makes very brief notes.

Once your minute is up, stand up, give your arms and legs a little shake, then sit down again in the same chair. Now close your eyes once more and briefly imagine that you're speaking in a 'normal' conversational way. When you've done this open your eyes again. Now it's time for your second run.

For your second run, step up a gear from your 'normal' conversation and speak for about a minute with a slightly higher level of commitment, fractionally more energy or urgency.

Once your minute is up, stand up, give your arms and legs a little shake, then sit down again in the same chair. As in Exercise 4, ask the observer to say what differences he or she saw in your body language and that of the listener.

We would expect the observer to report significant differences in body language and eye contact the second time round even though the difference between your two tasks is not as extreme as it was in Exercise 4. Behaviour will vary according to who is taking part, but some of the differences the observer might notice in the 'more committed' version are:

● you have put more emphasis on certain words

● you have spoken louder and/or faster

● you – and perhaps your listener too – have tended to sit further forward on your chair and/or to lean forward

● there has been more eye contact between you and your listener

● there has been more physical communication between you and your listener, such as gestures from you and nodding from your listener.

Maybe not all of these will show up, and there are many other possible differences. Whatever the precise observations, we are pretty sure that you will see greater interest and feedback from the listener when your level of commitment is higher.

We are also sure that the observer will give you feedback that will help you to develop your conscious awareness of the signs of success-ful communication. This conscious awareness will become, in time, an unconscious awareness – as it should be.

As before, when you have played your role as speaker, your friends can take their turn. You will learn something more from going through the speaker–listener–observer cycle again.

# Generating energy

Good communication generates
energy. You must have felt this
energy yourself when you've been in
an audience – at a concert, a sporting
event, a play, a political meeting, perhaps even a lecture.

There are many different kinds of energy:
excitement (tension), suspense (when the hairs
on the back of your neck stand up), good humour
(the bubbling-over kind), itchy feet (when you just
have to get up and dance), a sense of seriousness and
purpose (concern), paying attention (when you could
hear a pin drop). When presenting, you may want to
choose the kind of energy you want to generate – different
kinds, perhaps, at different points in your presentation. This is
probably something you know intuitively how to do, even if you
haven't had much experience of doing it in presentations. For
example, you would almost certainly generate one kind of energy in

the room if you were talking about the political situation in the Middle East and quite a different kind if you are telling a funny story.

Of course, there are different levels of energy. In an audience you might find yourself tremendously excited, moderately excited, a bit excited – or falling asleep. In some situations, when giving a presentation you might want to 'grow' the energy in the room, starting from a notch above conversational level and progressively raising it to a peak.

As a speaker, you kick-start the interaction between yourself and your audience by injecting energy into the proceedings. This requires effort from you, but once you've done it, you'll start to feel buoyed up by your audience's attention. In effect, *they* are now supplying *you* with energy.

We saw in the previous section (pages 18–23) that if you are strongly committed to handing over your message, this will automatically show in your body language and use of eye contact. Similarly, the more energy you are supplying, the more this too will automatically show, in the same way. Unlike commitment, though, you will probably want to 'ration' your energy.

If you did Exercises 4 and 5 (see pages 19–23), you've already experienced the energy difference between speaking in a normal conversational way and speaking with more energy or with less. Exercises 6, 7, 8 and 9 are designed to let you explore the kinds of energy you might use with a view to gaining control over your use of energy.

Exercise 6 – 'Exploring different kinds of energy' – may seem a long way from presentation. Indeed, it may also seem strange or even silly. As with all learning from experience, though, you need to try it before you judge it. Have a go – a serious try without holding back – and see what actually happens.

___

**Exercise 6: Exploring different kinds of energy**

*Purpose*
This is an exercise to accustom you to four different kinds of energy, and how they affect your bodily movements and facial expressions.

*Equipment*
Your imagination and a private, quiet room. Ideally you would have a friend to help you; it's important that this person is someone with whom you can be yourself, not someone who makes you feel self-conscious.

*What you do*

Most people find this exercise is best done standing up, though this is not absolutely necessary. To start, imagine that you are holding a ball in your hands – a ball of energy. If you have a friend with you, you will be passing this imaginary ball between the two of you. (If you're on your own, imagine your friend too!)

First of all, imagine that the ball is very heavy. As you hand it to and receive it from your friend, you will – if you are really feeling the weight – pass it slowly, carefully and steadily between you. Do this five or six times. Don't talk while you are doing it.

Now do the same thing with an imaginary ball of kinetic energy, pure speed. Feel it zipping around in your hands, and take care to control it as you hand it over and receive it.

Next, imagine that the ball has some thermal energy; it's nice and warm to the touch. Feel the warmth as you receive it and enjoy the comforting sensation you get as you wrap your hands around it.

Lastly, imagine that the ball in your hands is a diamond brooch. The workmanship is very fine and the brooch is light as a feather. When you pass it between you and your friend you must of course do it with great care.

When you've handled all four objects in turn, go through the sequence again. This time round, notice how the movements of your body and your facial expressions differ according to the ball that you're handling. With the heavy ball you'll probably brace yourself to receive it, and the look on your face and possibly a nod of your head will tell your friend when you feel you've got hold of it. When you're handing the ball over, the look on your face will probably be a quizzical one, silently asking your friend if it's safe for you to let go yet.

With that unpredictable ball of kinetic energy, you may well be concentrating on keeping your balance, and your face may show traces of puzzlement as you try to guess what it will do next and avoid being taken by surprise.

With the ball of thermal energy, you'll probably enjoy receiving it and holding it, and this will show: your body will be relaxed and your pleasure will show on your face.

And with that diamond brooch, your sense of the value and beauty of what you are handing over or receiving will probably make you careful and precise in your movements. Again, this will show on your face.

The next exercise involves working not with an imaginary ball but with a message, and using four kinds of energy – weight, speed, warmth and delicacy – in turn to 'power' your message.

### Exercise 7: Using energy to 'power' your message

*Purpose*
This is an exercise to help you learn how to use energy of different kinds to 'power' your communication.

*Equipment*
A private, quiet room, again with an actual or imaginary friend present.

*What you do*
To start with, you need a message, something to communicate. So choose a topic – we suggest *either* 'My best friend' *or* 'The King is dead' – and quickly jot down four brief points (one or two sentences each) on it. These four points comprise your message.

When you are ready, it's time to give your message. You're going to do this four times, using these four kinds of energy in turn. So you give your message first with weight, then with speed, then with warmth, then with delicacy, using the appropriate body movements and facial expressions each time. It may help to go back to the previous exercise before each message to remind yourself how that energy 'feels'.

You will almost certainly find that your message is easy to give with two out of the four kinds of energy, but not the other two. If you find that you're changing the wording of your message, it's a sure sign that the energy is of the wrong kind for your message. The lesson, then, is that whatever message you're going to be giving, you must make sure you give it with the right kind of energy. 'Right', by the way, means right for you, right for your subject matter and right for your audience.

Now that you've tried delivering your message with various different kinds of energy, there's one more kind we suggest you experiment with. Exercise 8 involves using 'concentrated' energy.

### Exercise 8: Discovering the effects of 'concentrated' energy

*Purpose*
This is an exercise to get you experimenting with the use of 'concentrated' energy.

*Equipment*
Your imagination, a private, quiet room, and – if possible – a partner. Don't tell your partner what you're doing, simply let them react to what you give them.

*What you do*
Most people find this exercise is best done standing up. To start, imagine – as in Exercise 6 – that you are holding an energy ball of speed or warmth in your hands. Pass it to and fro between you, without talking.

Get comfortable doing this . . . then, all of a sudden . . . change it! Now it's a FIRECRACKER!!!

Observe what reaction you get. (You may well get different reactions from different people.)

You may think that asking a presenter to deliver the energy of a firecracker is unrealistic, or even uncalled for. However, as you'll see later (pages 56–63), where we talk about grabbing attention, a firecracker is equivalent to a soundbite: something that grabs attention and can act as a 'wake-up call' for an audience.

The easiest way to generate energy in your performance as a presenter is through your attitude to your subject and material. If your subject excites you, let that excitement show by using the energy of 'speed'. If some aspect of your material makes you smile – perhaps it's a particularly neat explanation or leads to a humorous conclusion – then you can use the energy of 'warmth'.

Note that not only are certain kinds of energy likely to be better suited to certain subjects, they are also likely to be better suited to certain audiences and indeed, to be more comfortable for certain presenters. We suggest that you aim to develop your repertoire of 'energies', but don't let yourself be pushed into using kinds of energy that you don't feel comfortable with.

Finally, here is an exercise to help you discover and get used to the energy in your own voice. Not everybody needs this; if you are a member of a choir, or you like nothing better than taking part in a karaoke evening or shouting yourself hoarse at a football match, you are probably well accustomed to the energy in your voice already. But if these don't apply to you, and you shrink from the very idea, then try Exercise 9.

### Exercise 9: Discovering and getting used to the energy in your own voice

*Purpose*
This is an exercise to reduce the inhibitions that prevent you from coming out with energy in your voice.

*Equipment*
Somewhere private, preferably soundproofed, equipped with a music player or radio that you can turn up loud. A bathroom is a good place. If you drive, a car is even better. The fact that there is background noise – running water or noise from engine and wheels – will help.

*What you do*

If you're playing music, sing along. Take deep breaths and gradually – so as not to strain your voice – sing more and more loudly until you're singing at the top of your voice. If you hit a wrong note, or are completely out of tune, or run out of breath in the middle of a line – *it doesn't matter*. You have no audience. Just enjoy yourself, and get used to working your lungs and vocal chords.

If you're listening to a speech programme on the radio, heckle the speaker or speakers. Disagree with them. Abuse them. (You can be as rude as you like. There's no one else around to be shocked or to tell you off.) Raise your voice gradually until you're positively shouting at them. If you've never done this before you'll find it very therapeutic. Again, just enjoy yourself, and get used to working your lungs and vocal chords.

A by-product of doing this exercise is that when you're about to give a presentation, reminding yourself of your outrageous behaviour, whether singing or heckling, will certainly bring a smile to your face and reduce any anxiety you may be feeling.

# Part Two

# Preliminaries

# What is your brief?

As we reminded you in the Introduction, there are many different kinds of presentation, notably the academic presentation, the sales pitch, the job interview, the formal report and the after-dinner speech. There will always be a topic, and there will usually be a brief that tells you what you have to do with the topic. Often this is pretty straightforward: 'Highlight those qualities of the product that will appeal to this audience', 'Make sure you bring out your qualifications for the job', 'Go through the main items of expenditure and be sure to mention the benefits we got from each of them', and the famously pithy instruction to the best man at a wedding, 'Tell some jokes and read the telegrams'.

For academic presentations, however, matters may be less straightforward. Usually you will be assigned a topic, just as you would be for an essay. Your topic should be specific enough for you to start work on preparing a presentation of the kind that's wanted. For example, if your topic is in the form of a question you know that your job is to find the answer to that question, and to present it, together with the working by which you arrived at it. If you're told nothing more than 'Talk about X', the first thing you have to do is find something interesting about X and a way of bringing that out in your presentation. Sometimes the best way of doing that is to invent your own question. If that's what you do, it's sensible to check that it's a question your teacher is happy with.

Be aware, of course, that if your topic is worded in your subject's 'academicspeak' the first thing you will have to do is to interpret it, to translate it into language you can do something with. Say you're assigned the topic 'Is social exclusion a useful concept for understanding gendered dimensions of well-being in an international context?'. You have to start by (a) acknowledging that 'social exclusion' is a term used by different writers to mean different things, and choosing which you are going to use, and why; (b) deciding what you will take to be the meaning of the phrase 'gendered dimensions of well-being'; (c) being clear in your mind as to how a concept can be used 'for understanding'; and (d) appreciating the significance of the phrase 'in an international context'.

There is more to a brief than just a topic. Your topic is merely your starting point. How does your teacher expect you to deal with it? There are many different ways in which a topic can be tackled, and different teachers have different requirements. Yours may want one or more of the following:

- a review of the literature
- a reasoned answer to a set question
- a discussion of a proposition (a statement or quotation)
- an argument, incorporating your personal point of view.

Before you begin work on a presentation, you really, really *must* know what your brief is – how your teacher wants you to deal with the topic. This is something that your teacher should have made clear to you. Unfortunately, however, some teachers don't make it clear what it is they want. Their students are drawn into a guessing game. They put off starting work on the presentation while they cast around anxiously for clues about what they're expected to do. The day of the presentation gets closer and closer, and they get more and more stressed, and more and more doubtful of their academic ability. Some get depressed and some get ill. This is a scenario to be avoided.

The lesson for you is that if your teacher hasn't made it clear to you what you are expected to do, you must *ask*. First of all, ask your teacher face to face. If you don't get a clear answer, get out a pen and paper and ask what you should write down. You could show him or her the above bullet-point list and ask them to choose from it. If you are still not altogether clear, put together a very rough outline for a presentation – bullet points or headings will do – and give or email it to them, with questions like 'Will this do?', 'Have I left out anything I ought to put in?' At all costs, avoid being drawn into the guessing game.

You also need to know how much time you are allowed for your presentation. Five minutes? Ten? Twenty? Thirty? Again, if you aren't told, you must *ask*. There are few things worse than preparing a presentation and then, when you're halfway through giving it, getting signals from your teacher or your audience that it's time for you to wind up.

# Know your audience

## Five things about your audience that you need to think about

The audience has to be your first consideration in planning any presentation. There are five questions about your audience to which you absolutely must have answers, whatever kind of presentation you are going to give:

1. Who will be in the audience, and why will they be there?

2. Why does your audience need *this* presentation, about *this* subject?

3. What does your audience already know?

4. What kind of energy, on your part, will be appropriate to your audience?

5. What 'protocols' will you be expected to follow?

## Who will be in the audience, and why will they be there?

Even if your audience is a group that meets regularly, people may turn up for any of a variety of reasons. Some may attend because they really want to learn from you; some may turn up more in hope than anticipation, on the off-chance that they will pick up something valuable; others may come out of a sense of duty or because it will be noticed and held against them if they are absent. Those in the first category will want some 'meat' in your presentation; those in the second will appreciate a presentation that intrigues them; and those in the third would doubtless like to be entertained. Even if you decide to cater only for the first category, you need to be aware of the others, if only so that you won't be put off if they start getting fidgety.

As a student, you will often have to give presentations to mixed audiences. In a seminar you will usually be talking both to fellow students and to a teacher. If you are a research student presenting a paper at a conference, you may well find that your audience contains both fellow researchers, who are primarily interested in your research methods, and workers in industry who are primarily interested in your results and potentially marketable applications. In both cases, it will be sensible to incorporate something for everybody in your presentation.

## Why does your audience need *this* presentation, about *this* subject?

Your presentation will be all the more effective if you have been able to put yourself in your audience's position when creating your presentation. So ask yourself 'If I were in the audience, what would I need to gain from it? Why would this be of value to me?'.

## What does your audience already know?

The answer to this question may not be altogether straightforward. Your audience will have encountered information, ideas, perspectives and concepts during their course, but this does not necessarily mean that they 'know' them in the sense of being familiar with them. It will help you to ask yourself what you can take for granted that they are familiar with. This will give you a starting point, a 'foundation' on which you can 'build' your presentation.

Your audience's knowledge also comprises language: both the specialized language of the subject (technical language, jargon, 'academicspeak') and mother tongue. If you are a native English speaker who will be giving a presentation in English to an audience that you know will include people whose first language is not English, try to avoid using idiom, colloquialisms and unusual metaphors. If you do, your audience will get distracted: while you carry on talking, they'll be busy trying to translate what you're saying into language they can understand, so they won't be paying attention to what you're saying and you'll lose them. If you'll need to use specialized technical terms and acronyms that may be new to your audience (WTO for World Trade Organization, for example), you might like to provide a handout with a list of these.

## What kind of energy, on your part, will be appropriate to your audience?

Think of the different kinds of energy we explored earlier (see 'Generating energy', pages 24–30). Are you expected to be serious? Low-key? Can you be humorous or surprising?

## What 'protocols' will you be expected to follow?

'Protocols' are customs and conventions – rituals, even – that govern presentations like yours. In a context that is new to you, you need to ask about these. Will you be expected to answer questions after your presentation? In a conference or formal meeting, will you be expected to say polite things about your hosts or the previous speaker, or to make any additional remarks 'through the chair'? In a foreign country you need to take particular care to find out about such protocols, otherwise you are likely to embarrass your hosts, your audience and yourself, and embarrassment is not conducive to getting your message across.

If you don't know the answers to these five questions, you *must* ask the organizer of the event for the answers. In an ideal world he or she would brief you without you having to ask, but the world is not ideal. So if they don't, you will need to take the initiative. Don't be shy. Don't feel you ought to know the answers, or that it's up to you to guess them. Just go ahead and ask the five questions. If the answers aren't obvious, you are entitled to expect and ask for help from the organizer.

# The 'audience check'

Just as a band does a soundcheck before a gig, it can be very helpful for you to do an 'audience check' before you get going on your presentation. You can use some form of words like: 'I don't want to take up valuable time telling you things you already know, so can I just ask how many people here are familiar with X?' (Prepare one or two sentences along these lines, so you will have them ready.) Doing this not only gets you some valuable information, it also shows that you respect your audience, and they in turn will respect you. If your question reveals that half your audience *is* familiar with X but the other half is not, the better-informed half will be more tolerant than they otherwise might be of the time you spend describing or explaining X.

If you are a member of a group that meets regularly – one where you take it in turns to give presentations, for example – you'll already know who will be present in the audience, and why. But if they (or some of them) will be strangers it's crucial to get as much information about the likely audience as you can. You don't want to prepare something for your fellow students then find that your teacher has invited two distinguished professors along. Just as if in your working life you've prepared a presentation on travel in India for an audience of travel agents, then turn up to find that actually your audience is made up of eight-year-old schoolchildren, you're going to have to modify your presentation drastically on the spur of the moment.

Of course, in order to respond to whatever your audience check reveals you must be flexible. You have to be prepared to take some material quickly or slowly, depending on the answer you get. You may want to organize your material beforehand to cater for the least well informed, but have it in such a form that you can skip the more elementary bits if the audience doesn't need them.

# Clarify your goals and objectives

## Goals and objectives

We made the point in the Introduction (page 6) that presenters who are consistently successful invariably have *goals* and *objectives* clear in their minds. (A goal, remember, is something that we want to *achieve*, to bring about; an objective is something that we want to *do* – an action that we want to take – in order to achieve our goal.) One of your goals ought to be to hold your audience's attention; to that end your objectives might include the following:

- to speak in a language with which your audience is familiar
- to tell a story that will attract and hold their attention
- to provide a striking graphic to illustrate visually each of five main points that you want them to take away with them.

Of course, you can't actually *determine* that your audience will grasp and understand your five points, just as – we're told – you can lead a horse to water but you can't make it drink. What you are trying to do is to make it as easy and as enjoyable as possible for your audience to grasp and understand those points, and as rewarding as possible too. Learning from a presentation always calls for at least some effort from the audience. Your goals as a presenter should include encouraging them to make that effort and providing a reward for them when they do.

## Taking your cue from your audience

As we saw in the last section, 'Know your audience' (pages 36–39), different members of your audience are likely to want different things from your presentation. Some will want some 'meat', some will want to be intrigued, some would like to be entertained. If your goal is to provide all of these, your objectives could include:

- to provide a worthwhile amount of information and analysis, backed up by references
- to present a puzzle and take your audience through the detective work necessary to solve it
- to spice up your presentation with funny (but relevant) anecdotes.

Don't forget to ask yourself, 'If I were in the audience, what would I need to gain from it? Why would this be of value to me?' This might generate objectives such as:

- to spell out the underlying theories and principles employed
- to raise questions about existing 'knowledge' and suggest ideas for future research
- to highlight practical applications and show how needs can be met.

## How will you assess yourself?

Presenters have implicit goals too, goals that they tend to take for granted rather than consciously formulate – for example, the goal that the audience should form a favourable opinion of them. Not every presenter does have goals consciously in mind – if you are giving a presentation because you are compelled to do so, your one thought may be to get the ordeal over – but here are two that you might like to adopt for yourself:

1. One of my top goals is to do myself justice – to do justice to the work I've put in to preparing for this presentation

2. Another of my top goals is to learn from all my experiences of giving presentations.

Even the most skilled and experienced presenters sometimes mess up. However, they don't go away and shoot themselves or retire from public life; they say to themselves, 'Ho hum. I didn't really do justice to myself there! How can I do better next time?' It's a healthy attitude. Make it yours too.

# How will you be assessed?

There's no escaping the fact that as a presenter you are going to be judged – assessed – by your audience. Assessment of student presentations is an established feature of higher education today: a Google search for 'presentation assessment' reveals hundreds of assessment forms and instructions used at a variety of universities and colleges. Each one offers its own particular set of criteria for assessing your presentation. In general, these criteria fall into two categories:

1.  Academic criteria, such as use of literature, understanding of subject, organization of material
2.  'Quality of communication' criteria, such as audibility, use of visual aids and keeping to time.

Academic criteria in particular vary greatly, among subjects and institutions; consequently it's beyond the scope of this book to deal with them. There's less variation among 'quality of communication' criteria, but using them presents a problem. For example, you may be given a 'presentation assessment sheet' with a section headed 'Quality of communication' in which the stated criteria are:

- audibility, liveliness and clarity of presentation
- confidence and fluency in use of English
- appropriate use of body language (inc. eye contact)
- listening skills – responsiveness to audience.

What on earth can you do with this list? Well, you could aim to translate each of these criteria into an objective, but try it and you'll find that it's a far from straightforward thing to do because you are given no hint as to the standard you are expected to achieve.

You could have a shot at turning these criteria into questions. This might give you:

- Can I be heard clearly at the back of the room? Do I express myself in a way that is reasonably 'conversational', using pauses and emphasis to help get my points over, rather than (say) 'woodenly' reading out the notes I have prepared?
- Do I use words correctly? Is my grammar correct?
- Do I move my arms and body about appropriately, rather than (say) staying fixed and immobile in one position? Do I look at the audience often enough?
- Can I understand the questions that come from the audience, and give sensible answers to them?

Here it is a little bit clearer what you should be aiming at, but the standards are still vague, because they necessarily involve subjective judgments on the part of the assessor (a consequence of the fact that communication is a 'soft' skill, not one reducible to following 'hard' rules).

Clearly it would be a fine thing if you could confidently answer 'yes' to all the above questions. But if you have never given a presentation before, you could be excused for finding them highly intimidating. They are almost guaranteed to make you self-conscious and get you worrying – about your audibility, about your use of English, about your movements, about whether you will be able to understand questions that are put to you. Issuing such a list is like telling someone who's learning to ride a bike to lean inwards at an angle of 27 degrees when going round a corner. Worrying about whether you've got the angle right – thinking consciously about what you are doing rather than trying it out – is a surefire recipe for falling off! So unless you are starting out with great confidence, paying attention to such a list of assessment criteria and worrying about them can be highly counterproductive.

Some assessment criteria are more 'concrete'. If you are going to be assessed on 'keeping to time' and are told you have 20 minutes for your presentation, there is no subjective judgment involved: you know exactly what you have to do. So pay attention to these criteria and do your best to meet them.

Our advice, then, is that when you are starting out on learning to give presentations, you should positively ignore any 'quality of communication' assessment criteria you are given that are not concrete or that can't be translated into concrete terms. Once you have got started, and have a few presentations under your belt, by all means look at such lists then to see what scope you have for improving. In Part Eight of this book – 'Evaluation' – we'll return to this subject and help you to use such lists to draw useful lessons for next time. Meanwhile, formulate your own goals and objectives for specific presentations along the lines suggested earlier in this section, and concentrate on the message you want to give your audience and the points you would like them to take away.

# Observe other people's presentations

In your daily life as a student, you are likely to be repeatedly exposed to two particular kinds of presentation given by other people: the lecture, delivered by one of your teachers, and the 'paper' given in a seminar, class or group tutorial by one of your fellow students. Repeated exposure to such presentations will almost certainly 'condition' you to take it for granted that this is the example you should follow when you yourself give a presentation. Being conditioned to take things for granted is not an effective way of learning to be a good presenter. Instead, start off by making careful observations and trying out techniques, then practise the techniques you want to emulate until you have internalized them, so they become second nature to you.

# The lecture

Think back to the various lectures you've attended. Some may have struck you as bad ones. You may recognize some of the features of bad presentations that we listed on page 2. They almost amount to a recipe for giving a really bad presentation.

Now think about the lectures that have struck you as good ones. Can you say *why* they struck you as good? Were they easy to follow? Easy to take notes in? Informative? Entertaining? Were you given helpful handouts?

Next, think about the various *lecturers* you've seen and listened to. Have some of them been better than others? Can you say what the characteristics of a good lecturer are? (Be more specific than 'someone who gives good lectures'.) Is it someone who doesn't go too fast? Someone who checks frequently that their audience has understood the point they've just made? Someone who doesn't 'talk down' to their audience? Someone who looks at their audience, rather than keeping their eyes fixed on their notes or delivering a monologue in the direction of the ceiling?

These questions may not be easy ones to answer, especially if you've been concentrating on taking notes in their lectures. If you do find them difficult to answer, we suggest that you compare your impressions with those of your fellow students. Next time you attend a lecture, arrange with them that one or two of you don't take notes but instead concentrate on observing how the lecturer behaves. Take note of such things as speaking speed and pauses; repetition of words or phrases, or of points made using different language; body movements and gestures, extent of eye contact made with the audience. Notice how the lecture is organized, structured. Does it start with a question and progress logically to the answer, for example, or does it consist of a 'tour' of aspects of a theme, say? If it is offered as an 'argument', how does the lecturer construct an argument?

After the lecture, compare your observations and see if you can work out what bits of behaviour made the lecture – as a whole or in parts – 'good' or 'bad'. When you've done that, think about which of them you might be able to adopt for yourself when you give a presentation. First, though, you need to work out which ones 'worked' because they were given by someone who was thoroughly knowledgeable about the subject, who was able to speak with authority, who was an experienced lecturer. These are three features that you, as a student, simply do not have (unless you're a PhD student within a year or so of submitting your thesis). It will be fatal to your own presentation to pretend to have knowledge, authority and experience that you do not possess. By all means follow examples of helpful handouts and easy-to-follow structures, and good style in making eye contact with your audience, but don't follow examples that are not appropriate for students.

## Other students' presentations

Just as with lectures, notice what you find good and what you find not so good about the presentations that your fellow students give. As with lectures, try to correlate your judgments with such things as speaking speed and pauses; repetition of words or phrases, or of points made using different language; body movements and gestures, extent of eye contact made with the audience. Again, notice how each presentation is structured.

You can now try out good techniques, look back at presentations you yourself have given recently, and see whether there are things you did well – pat yourself on the back for these – and others where you would do things differently next time. After you've tried the exercises we are suggesting in this book, do some more observing of other people's presentations. This will help you to get a clearer idea of what works, and *why* it works.

# Part Three

# Preparing your materials

# Do your homework, think about your topic and decide your plan

Doing your homework, thinking about your topic and deciding your plan are constituent strands of any academic process that involves working with words. They take place simultaneously, 'in parallel'. Table 1 gives an idea of how they might progress together.

We have a few suggestions to offer here.

- Do *not*, under any circumstances, start by attempting to 'read' through all the publications on your reading list in the conventional way, one after the other, page by page. You'll get bogged down in a mass of irrelevant material; you'll get bored and frustrated, especially if you have to do a lot of translating of 'academicspeak' into language you can understand; and you'll end up running out of time and feeling completely unprepared to give your presentation.

Table 1: The academic process

| Doing your homework | Thinking about your topic | Deciding your plan |
|---|---|---|
| Perusing your reading list and getting hold of publications (books, articles, official reports, etc.) on the list | Puzzling out what your brief requires you to do | Choosing a principle for your plan, e.g. question to answer, series of aspects of a theme, or argument |
| Sorting through publications to find material (e.g. theoretical work, research results, discussion, empirical data) that is relevant to your topic | Interpreting your topic and clarifying the meanings you should give to technical or colloquial terms | Roughing out a draft plan in general terms, using headings, e.g. Introduction/Materials/ Methodology/ Discussion/Conclusion or Introduction/Aspect 1/Aspect 2/Aspect 3/ Summary/Conclusion |
| Careful reading to familiarize yourself with relevant passages | (a) Critical reading of relevant material to identify, e.g. disagreements between writers, faulty reasoning; making notes (b) Finding an 'angle' that interests or even enthuses you | |
| | (a) Returning to the topic to make sure you have understood it correctly (b) Identifying the methodology you want to use (e.g. to arrive at the answer to a question) and selecting the material you will apply it to (e.g. empirical data and writings); making notes | Updating your plan, inserting subheadings, bearing in mind that it will need to follow your reasoning in its final form, e.g. your progression from question to answer |
| Checking out the publications you have used to ensure you haven't overlooked or misunderstood something significant | Actually applying your methodology to your material; making notes | Reviewing your plan in the light of your notes, and updating it if necessary |
| | | Modifying your plan to make it suitable for verbal presentation (as opposed to an essay) |

You will only make matters worse if you try to go through a mass of publications taking detailed notes and/or highlighting passages without having a clear idea of what is relevant. This is a very time-consuming process.

● When doing your initial sorting through publications, equip yourself with a stack of Post-its to use as bookmarks. When you come across something that might be relevant, don't get seduced into reading but stick a Post-it on the page so you can easily find the place again later.

● Pay close attention to the precise wording of your topic. (Just as in examinations, you *must* answer the question: academics are very hot on this.) It will probably help you, both in focusing your reading and in interpreting the topic, to make a list of the key words from your topic: these could be either technical terms or colloquial ones.

● If your teacher wants a review of the literature, you could either go through the publications one by one, and present a short summary of each one by one, or you could identify certain recurring aspects or themes in the literature and, in your presentation, deal with the aspects or themes one by one. The former approach is a weak one; the latter is a strong one, because you will get more deeply into the subject matter – you will be identifying differences between the various writings (the authors make different assumptions, or different judgments, or they use different theories, or they draw their evidence from different sources, for example), and you will find yourself thinking critically, which always impresses academics.

● If your teacher wants a reasoned answer to a set question, you need to ask yourself: 'How can I tell – how can I work out – what the answer to the question is?' Then you can present the sequence of steps by which you have got from question to answer (just as you would if the question required you to find the solution to a mathematical problem). In general your steps should lead you from what is known to what is unknown: from empirical evidence and established 'facts' and theories to 'what would happen if ...'.

● If your teacher wants a discussion of a proposition (a statement or quotation), a helpful approach is to turn this into a question: 'Is it accurate (or valid) to say that ...?' Then you can continue as if this were a set question to which a reasoned answer is required, as in the above example.

● If your teacher wants you to present an argument, incorporating your personal point of view, there are a number of possibilities. (a) You could start by presenting two or more alternative points of view, then say which you prefer, giving your reasons. (b) You could start by setting out a single point of view, then list what you see as points for it and points against (pros and cons), and conclude by saying whether you think the points for outweigh the points against, or vice versa. (c) If you are making a critique of someone else's argument, you could first state or summarize the argument, then pull it apart into its constituent elements, analyse and criticize each of these in turn, then offer your judgment as to its value, or the value that it would have if it were modified in some respects. (d) You could state your point of view at the outset, go on to back it up with whatever evidence, authoritative opinion or comment you can lay your hands on, and conclude by restating your point of view. This last approach does not provide you with any kind of logical structure: it is intellectually sloppy and consequently to be avoided at all costs, although you may well encounter it in lectures that you attend. A good principle is to hold back your personal judgments until you have reviewed all the evidence, literature etc., which you do as impartially and objectively as you can.

(Unfortunately there are some teachers who will set you a question and then say something like: 'I want to see a strong argument from you.' Be aware that this is a recipe for sowing confusion in your mind. A question calls for an *answer*, not an argument. Explaining (if it's a 'Why?' question) requires a completely different mindset from arguing. Working from question to answer is something that you do in logical steps, like solving a problem (whether or not creativity is required). But if you start drafting your presentation by stating a question, then go on to say 'I'm going to argue that ...', you're in a quandary as to what you do next. There is no evident sequence of steps to follow, hence your confusion. If a teacher of yours sets you a question and asks you to respond with an argument, don't fall into the trap and feel you have to provide one. The safe thing to do in this situation is to state your conclusion at the outset – 'I shall show that there are good grounds for saying that the answer to this question is X' – and then go back to the question and take your audience through your reasoning from question to answer.)

In this section we have dealt with the processes of doing your homework, thinking about your topic and deciding your plan in a way that will meet conventional academic requirements. Indeed, the combination of processes is one that you could use if you were planning an essay. When you have to give a presentation, however, what you have is no more than a fleshed-out plan. You have to take the process further. Remember that the very last item in Table 1, under the heading 'Deciding your plan', is 'Modifying your plan to make it suitable for verbal presentation (as opposed to an essay)'. Ways of doing this are outlined in the next section, 'Make your message memorable'. You will also be augmenting your plan with visual aids and handouts, if you are going to use them, and providing yourself with 'prompts'. Prompts can take the form of a sequence of index cards, notes on particular points, annotated printouts of slides or even a full script; their purpose is to enable you to give your presentation confidently and clearly. These are the subjects of the remaining sections of this part of the book.

# Make your message memorable

As a presenter, you want the most important parts of your message to stick in the audience's minds. You want to make your message memorable. It's a good idea to grab your audience's attention at the outset and grab it again each time you want to reinforce a point. How can you do this? Here are some suggestions:

- Begin by saying something arresting
- Communicate your engagement with the topic
- Tell a story
- Give your audience an agenda ('route map')
- Use soundbites
- Repeat important points
- Have a neat, punchy ending.

Ideally you would do all of these. If that looks likely to require a lot of preparation, don't worry: just a few basic principles are involved. You will be familiar with these principles in an unconscious way, because you see, read or hear stories that communicate information every day in newspapers and magazines, on TV, and in books or even other presentations.

## Begin by saying something arresting

Here are some ways to make an audience sit up and take notice right from the start:

● Disagree with something you've read: 'X says there is only one way to . . . I disagree.'

● Offer a puzzle or paradox: 'In some cities, the rich people live in the centre and the poor people live on the outskirts. In others, it's exactly the opposite: the poor people live in the centre and the rich people live on the outskirts. How can we explain this difference?'

● Offer a striking fact: 'In Britain today, two out of every five marriages end in divorce.'

● Surprise your listeners with a relevant quote from an unlikely non-academic source: Homer Simpson, for example.

● Just state your conclusion, and then ask the rhetorical question: 'What leads me to this conclusion?'

A good thing about beginning by saying something arresting is that your body language and use of your eyes are likely to match what you're saying. If you're saying something arresting you are likely to be behaving in an arresting way: holding yourself upright and looking at your audience face to face(s). Much better than hunching over your script or notes and looking at those rather than at the people in front of you.

## Communicate your engagement with the topic

You want your audience to engage with your topic, with the subject matter of your presentation. It will help you to do this if you can communicate to them your own engagement with it. So tell your audience what excited or surprised you in your research on this topic – and why. Tell them what question you really wanted to find an answer to – and why it was so important. What was the most difficult thing to understand? It is easy to fall into the trap of thinking that academic presentations should be about facts, theories and ideas, and that your feelings about your material have no place. But, in fact, this is how your topic can be brought to life – and thereby made to matter in the lives of your audience.

## Tell a story

We have all known since childhood that telling a story keeps an audience interested from one moment to the next. What are the characteristics of a good story? Here are some suggestions.

- It is often based on a logical, chronological sequence of events (although some good stories incorporate flashbacks). There's a 'timeline', so to speak. The story 'unfolds' along the time dimension: it carries the audience along with it.

- It keeps the audience hooked, in suspense. They want to know what happens next. What's the outcome? Is there a happy ending?

- It intrigues the audience. It offers puzzles that engage their minds. They want to know the solutions to these puzzles.

- There are one or more characters with whom members of the audience identify. These are usually people, but they can be organizations (those whose goals are shared by the audience), teams (think of football teams), celebrities (whether in public life or in the specific field of the presentation), or even brands.

Each of these is a method by which stories have been told since the dawn of time. They create 'narrative'. Your next sentence may not be attention-grabbing in itself, but it holds attention because of what has gone before, and what might come later. It holds attention because of the context.

These narrative tricks don't all have to be present in a good story, but you can see one or more of them used in any novel or TV drama – and also in jokes, in magazine articles, in case studies . . . and in presentations!

There is one unique story you can tell in a presentation that uses all these narrative tricks. If you are telling the story of how you tackled your topic, you will have all four of these ingredients: timeline, suspense, intrigue and a narrator – yourself – with whom your fellow students should be able to identify. (No doubt they too have had, or will have, presentations to give.) You can tell your audience how you interpreted the topic, how you worked out what material you needed and/or what sources you had to consult, how you reasoned your way to your conclusion, what problems you encountered en route, what issues your exploration, investigation or review raised for you. You could have a really good story to tell.

We strongly recommend that you at least consider using this particular story when giving your presentation. It does have the great further benefit that you don't have to pretend to be an authority on the subject. You can be yourself: a student, a person striving to learn. As far as we're concerned, the status of 'student' is an honourable one, not one with connotations of ignorance and inferiority. If you are making an honest attempt to learn, and showing this in your story, you will be deserving of nothing but respect.

This particular story has yet another benefit. You can 'flag up' any or all of the problems you encountered as items for discussion. So if your presentation is going to be followed by a discussion, you'll be offering a ready-made agenda for the discussion part of the proceedings.

## Give your audience an agenda ('route map')

Some people in your audience will think of your presentation in a chrono-logical way, as a sequence of statements made over a period of time, however short. For others, your presentation is like a journey: a journey into unfamiliar territory, perhaps, or taking a new route through territory they already know quite well. Whatever the way in which they view your presentation, they are likely to appreciate an agenda or route map for it.

There's a famous piece of advice to presenters which goes like this:

1. Tell them what you're going to tell them.
2. Then tell them.
3. Then tell them what you've told them.

In effect, there are three stages: (1) introduction; (2) exposition; (3) summary.

Telling them what you're going to tell them doesn't necessarily mean you should give away all your interesting bits right at the beginning! In stage 1, your introduction, you simply describe how your presentation is going to be structured: 'First I will say why the subject of social exclusion is topical and important. I will then demonstrate that different writers give different meanings to this term, and say which one I prefer, and why. Next I will show how the concept of social exclusion can help us to understand how differences in well-being among different groups in the population come about. Finally, I will suggest some of the policy implications that follow from this understanding.'

This brief introduction tells listeners to expect four clearly defined sections to your presentation, in a logical sequence. (In terms of the journey, you will visit four areas one after another.) This introduction will help the audience to know 'where they are' from moment to moment, and 'where they are going'.

In stage 2, your exposition, you actually go through the four sections in sequence, or 'visit' the four areas in turn.

In stage 3, your summary, you can look back and give a short version of your sequence of points. It's as if you show your audience a map of the journey they've taken and quickly trace the route with your finger. Just as a map looks different once you have completed your journey – lines, colours and symbols have a new significance for you – reviewing your agenda or route map is likely to add to your audience's understanding. Your summary can highlight crucial points in a way that your introduction couldn't, because in your introduction you did not want to give away your key points. At the end, of course, you want people to go away remembering those points, even if they don't remember all the detail and reasoning that held them together.

## Use soundbites

Soundbites are concise, pithy, easily understood phrases or sentences that encapsulate a message. Politicians (or their speech writers), headline writers and advertising people are dab hands at producing them, although their use to put a 'spin' on uncomfortable news or to convey a half-truth is not unknown.

However, used honestly, soundbites are a valuable tool for the presenter. Think of them as attention-grabbers, wake-up calls. They have a concentrated energy, like a firecracker. They get audiences interested. (As you would expect, a soundbite can also serve as an arresting opening statement.) And they are handy for summing up a section of your presentation and opening up a new one.

You don't need to have a way with words to come up with great soundbites. Creativity can be learned. First you need to understand the principles behind soundbites. Table 2 gives examples.

Table 2: The principles behind creating soundbites

| Principle | Soundbite |
|---|---|
| Offer a paradox or seeming contradiction that calls for an explanation | 'Gunmen tire of carrying guns.' (Topic: Can violence in Northern Ireland be ended?) |
| Challenge conventional wisdom | 'Sex doesn't always sell.' (Topic: An advertising campaign that flopped) |
| Play on words | 'You can upgrade your life.' (Topic: Appraisal of the benefits of new computer technology) |
| Use a familiar saying in an unusual/ unexpected context | 'Thrown in at the deep end.' (Topic: Burial at sea) |
| Make a personal appeal to your audience | 'Your country needs you!' (Topic: How to protect the environment) |
| Highlight a sensational fact (sex, death, big/little money, scandal, violence) | 'Killed for £3.25.' (Topic: The nature of drug-related crime) |
| Name recognition (famous person, brand name, team or organization) | 'Bill Gates will be worried.' (Topic: Downturn in the computer industry) |

You can use any of these principles to create your soundbites. If your imagination falters, do a bit of brainstorming. Think about the various 'ingredients' of your topic, and ask yourself six crucial questions: Who? What? Where? When? Why? How?

Write down your answers to these questions (it doesn't matter if one or two aren't applicable). Now ask yourself which of these answers would be of most interest to your particular audience. This should yield a little list of two or three things that it would be really good to get into your soundbite.

Now remind yourself of the principles listed in Table 2, and scrutinize your little list carefully to see if you can find a paradox or contradiction, something that challenges conventional wisdom, an amusing play on words, a contentious or argumentative assertion, a sensational fact or a familiar saying that you can apply in an unusual or unexpected context. Do a little brainstorming. Treat it as playtime. Paradoxically, the more fun you have with the ideas the more likely it is that a soundbite will occur to you.

## Repetition

This is a narrative trick specifically for verbal storytelling.

One thing that most of us are taught (perhaps unconsciously) when learning to write English is that we should not repeat words. Indeed, it is regarded as good style to vary one's language. So you might come across the following advice on essay writing: 'A good essay is concise. The best compositions have a message for the reader. A piece of writing that does not have a clear structure is difficult to follow.'

In contrast, when you're making an oral presentation it can be a good idea to repeat words and be consistent in your phrasing. Doing this helps to get an idea to stick. We can illustrate this with the above example. Read the following aloud:

A good essay has three attributes. One, a good essay is concise. Two, a good essay has a message for the reader. Three, a good essay has a clear structure that makes it easy to follow.

Notice that (a) the opening sentence is preparing the listener for the 'threesome' that is to follow; (b) the repetition of 'a good essay' provides a rhythm, and this makes it easier both to say and to listen to (rather like poetry); (c) all three attributes (not just two) are expressed positively; and (d) the listener won't be distracted into wondering whether an essay is the same as a composition and a piece of writing, or whether there are differences.

## Have a neat, punchy ending

When you start a presentation you need a soundbite: a stand-alone, attention-grabbing sentence or phrase. Your ending can be striking either in itself (another stand-alone soundbite) or because of its place in the story, its context. So the strategies for producing good endings are a mixture of soundbite and narrative strategies:

- *Bullets.* If your summary – 'Tell them what you've told them' – consists of a handful of crucial points, you can remind your audience of these in a concise, concentrated form as bullet points. The soundbite strategies may help you to do this. You may, of course, repeat soundbites from earlier in your presentation.

- *Come full circle.* This is a favourite narrative trick, much used by magazine articles. Suppose you started with a specific example, a mini case study, before going on to discuss the general principles of your topic. You might want to return to that specific example: 'What does all this mean for Paul Robertson, the farmer I spoke about at the beginning of the presentation? Well, now we can see that he could have avoided disaster by doing any one of four things . . .'. Similarly, if you started your presentation by posing a question, it is always sound to return to the question at the end, when you offer your answer to it along with any conditions and qualifications that need to be attached to it and any implications that follow from it.

- *Draw strands together.* If your presentation has taken the form of a 'tour' of aspects of a topic, do your best to bring them together in some way – for example, by bringing out common features or significant differences. Such an overview demonstrates that you can see the 'bigger picture', and usually goes down well with academics.

- *Pose a new question, or put forward a proposal*: 'Now we know what happens when . . ., what can we do to make sure it never happens again?' This is both a narrative and a soundbite trick. It says: 'The story goes on, and *you* should be thinking about what happens next.'

# Visual aids

## Why use visual aids?

To begin by stating the obvious, 'visuals' – material conveyed by means of visual aids – can communicate a different kind of information from that conveyed in speech. A diagram, graph, pie chart, histogram or picture can communicate information in a form that the (tutored) eye can take in very rapidly. The number of words required to spell out this information would be so great as to constitute a huge and probably indigestible mass. Even if your visual consists only of text – two or three bullet points, say – you can use it to complement and reinforce your speech: to remind your audience of the structure of your presentation and the point you've reached in it. The best presentations make good use of both words and visuals, and are all the more effective and striking for doing so.

For you as a presenter, it is the combination of visual and spoken communication, engaging eyes as well as ears, that is a particularly potent one. Whatever the form of the visual, showing it along with speech can get your message over in a way that speech alone cannot.

There is an important caveat here, however. Diagrams, graphs, pie charts and histograms are in effect conveying information in another language, a specialized language, a language that is quite different from English or any other spoken language. Even if your audience is familiar with the language, you should regard it as your responsibility to assist them in comprehending what you are conveying and to confirm that they are translating it correctly into English (or whatever language you are working in).

## What's available?

There are many kinds of visual aid media that can be used to complement the spoken element of a presentation. The ones in most common use today are:

- *whiteboard* (usually wall-mounted; the successor to the blackboard, using dry-wipe markers instead of chalk)
- *flipchart* (a pad of paper of A1 size – eight times the size of A4 – fixed at its top edge to an easel)
- *overhead projector (OHP)* (used for projecting A4-size transparencies – alias acetates, foils and write-on films – on to a screen or light-coloured wall)
- *PowerPoint* and other computer-generated slides (usually projected on to a screen)
- *video* (movie sequences, nowadays often created and projected digitally using a computer).

There are of course other media, such as film (on reels shown using a film projector and screen, as in a cinema) and 35 mm slides (often mounted in a carousel and shown using a slide projector). Today, however, these tend to be used only for specialized purposes, and accordingly we concentrate on the five 'general purpose' media listed above.

# Which medium to choose?

Each of the five visual aid media (whiteboard, flipchart, OHP, PowerPoint and video) has its own particular pros and cons – advantages and dis-advantages, suitability and unsuitability for different situations. We have listed these in Table 3.

**Table 3: The pros and cons of different visual aid media**

| Medium | Pros | Cons |
|---|---|---|
| Whiteboard | In comparison with a flipchart sheet, a whiteboard can accommodate more material and/or larger handwriting, and is easier to read from the back of a large room. Good for putting up brief notes and rough, not-too-complicated diagrams, including the products of brainstorming with your audience. Complex diagrams or long sentences *can* be created, but only if there are elements of anticipation and surprise to keep your audience hooked. | Whiteboards are usually mounted on the wall facing the audience and behind the speaker, so you have your back to your audience while you are writing or drawing. Despite this, you can hold the attention of an audience if you don't take too long and if you can keep them curious about what comes next; suspense is invaluable to a presenter! It is very tempting to put more material on the board than is necessary. Consider putting ancillary material, such as web addresses and references to sources, on a handout instead of writing it on the board. If you have little or no experience of writing on a whiteboard, you will find it very difficult to keep your lines of writing horizontal and the size of your letters uniform. The handwriting of someone who is unused to whiteboards is often very difficult to read. At the end of your session you have to clean the board, and the material cleaned off is lost. If you fill the board before the end of the session, time and your audience's attention are lost while you clean it. |
| Flipchart | The easel can be moved around. A place may be found where you can write on it without turning your back on your audience (cf. whiteboard). Sheets can be prepared in | The relatively small area of a flipchart sheet limits the amount of material that can be placed on it. (Some presenters get round this by tearing off 'used' sheets and displaying them poster-fashion in the room.) Because sheets |

| Medium | Pros | Cons |
|---|---|---|
| | advance. Used sheets can be saved, thereby preserving the material on them. A clean sheet is obtained in an instant by simply turning over the used ones. Good for putting up brief notes and rough, not-too-complicated diagrams, including the products of brainstorming with your audience. | are relatively small they may be difficult to read from the back of a large room. |
| OHP | Transparencies can readily be created in advance using a printer and/or printed copy and a photocopier. They can also be created by hand on the spot using special pens, which are available in a wide variety of colours. Transparencies can be shown in any order. | Care is needed in handling transparencies – they are supplied interleaved with tissue paper – and in lining them up on the projector table so that a vertical line on the transparency shows as a vertical line on the screen, for example. Aligning transparencies usually has to be done one by one, and by hand. A printer and/or printer and photocopier are needed to produce professional-looking transparencies. OHP lamps are liable to overheat and burn out, especially in older models. |
| PowerPoint | Suitable for both complex and simple slide content. Showing is very straightforward, once the equipment is set up. Moving through the sequence of slides involves no more than pressing a single key. It is very simple and straightforward to print out the slides to make a handout. It is possible to incorporate video clips and animation, and illustrations that change in real time, in a slide show. | Because the slides are pre-prepared, it is pretty much impossible to make changes during a presentation. You may be tempted to indulge in animation – 'bells and whistles' – which detract from rather than add to your presentation: form triumphs over content. Not suitable for activities that involve contributions from your audience. |
| Video | If the subject of your presentation is the 'real world', video can convey it to your audience with great impact. | Video is a very demanding medium: a video produced by an amateur usually strikes the audience as amateurish. |

# Using visual aids

Here we offer you some exercises to develop your skill in using visual aids. Even if you are not due to make a presentation in the near future, you can do these exercises with diagrams, graphs, pie charts, histograms or tables from textbooks or other publications. Note that what you are doing is translating from the 'language' of the diagram, or whatever, into the English language. This is an extremely important skill to have in subjects like economics, where you are in effect using four languages – ordinary English, 'economics-speak', the language of graphs and the language of equations – and need to become proficient in shifting rapidly between them if you are to do well (part of learning to think like an economist).

Exercise 10 is an exercise in reading and translating visuals. By 'reading' we mean identifying what is significant in them, as in 'reading the signs'. The essence of the exercise is to describe, in a sequence that runs from language (the terms used) to the factual (descriptive) to the significant (the features which you want your audience to grasp) to inferences (what you consider to require explaining, or to be good or bad, etc.). If you leave out any of the steps in this sequence, you run the risk that your audience will be unable to follow you.

### Exercise 10: Reading and translating visuals

*Purpose*
This is an exercise to develop your fluency in reading and translating visuals.

*Equipment*
Somewhere quiet (a desk in a library or your own room will be fine), and one or more textbooks and/or journal articles containing a selection of diagrams etc. You don't actually need visual aid equipment for this exercise.

*What you do*
Let's say you have come across a graph showing average UK house prices over the past 50 years. You make the following notes for speaking, for what you would say if you were actually showing this graph as a visual to an audience as part of a presentation.

1.  A one-line introduction to the 'language' of the diagram: what the diagram shows. For example, 'This graph shows how the average price of houses in the UK varied year by year from the fourth quarter of 1952 to the fourth quarter of 2004.'

2.  A factual statement that provides an 'orientation' for your prospective audience: 'The y-axis is calibrated in thousands of pounds, from £1000 to £160,000. The x-axis is calibrated in years, from 1952 to 2004. The line on the graph connects up the points that represent the average UK house price in each three-month period.'

3.  Features that you consider to be significant (your reading of the graph): 'First, notice the sheer scale of the increase that has taken place: from almost £1900 in 1952 to almost £154,000 in 2004. The average UK house price at the end of 2004 was more than 80 times the average price at the end of 1952. Second, notice that there have been periods of very rapid increase (shown by the steepness of the line on the graph): 1971–74, 1978–80, 1988–89, and 2002–04. And, third, notice that there have been periods when the average UK house price fell: there was a fall in 1954; but the next fall wasn't until 36 years later, over the period 1990–92; prices remained fairly level during 1993–95 and did not begin to rise again until 1996.'

4.  Your inferences, leading on to the next part of your presentation: 'There are three features that call for explanation: the sheer scale of the overall increase, the periods of steep increase, and the fall in the 1990s after 36 years of continuous growth', *or* 'How can a house price "crash" be avoided now?', *or* 'The growth of owner occupation has clearly been a good thing because it has made many people wealthy.'

Notice how your spoken words complement your visual in different ways. Not only do they add to it by bringing out the significant features that you want to concentrate on, they also reinforce it by repeating some of the words on the slide. Don't regard such repetition as unnecessary: when you are reading aloud what your audience is reading silently at the same time, they will feel 'accompanied', that you are with them. And of course the combination of identical visual and spoken messages will make a stronger impression than either one alone: they're 'aligned', together they carry more 'energy'.

# Choosing a pointer

One of the main ways in which you keep your audience focused is by literally pointing to the salient features of your visual. There are several means of doing this: holding a long 'stick' up to a screen; shining a beam from a laser pen; holding a pen or pencil to an OHP transparency; highlighting a section of a PowerPoint slide. Try to avoid having to use your hand as a pointer: this looks amateurish and your audience will think you are unprepared. Here are some suggestions that may help in choosing a pointer.

## Stick

This requires you to stand close to the screen and to one side of it. An advantage is that both you and your audience are focused on the same point on the screen. Possible disadvantages are (a) you may have difficulty in finding a place to stand where you don't obstruct someone's view; and (b) a long stick can be unwieldy if not made of a light material.

## Laser pen

Again an advantage is that both you and your audience are focused on the same point on the screen, and because you don't need to stand close to the screen it may be easier than with a stick to avoid obstructing anyone's view. Possible disadvantages are (a) if your hand is shaking at all this will be apparent to your audience; and (b) the point where the laser beam strikes the screen may be too small for everybody to see easily.

## Pen or pencil placed on top of an OHP transparency

This is fairly easy to use, but has three potential disadvantages: (a) you may well find that you are obstructing someone's view; (b) the pointer is magnified in the same way as the transparency, and may obscure details of the visual; and (c) you are giving your attention to the transparency while the audience is concentrating on the screen, so if they look at you they are not referred back to the visual.

## Highlighting a section of a PowerPoint slide

This can be very effective if it is done well, but has three disadvantages: (a) it requires a lot of preparation if you want to make a complex point; (b) you have no flexibility – you're 'tied' to showing exactly what you have prepared; and (c) highlighting can look 'flashy' to the point of being distracting if not used with some subtlety.

# Make sure your visuals are audience-friendly

For maximum audience-friendliness, all your visuals should be self-explanatory, as far as possible. That's to say, it should be clear what each visual is showing, without any commentary from you. Your job will be to point out the *significance* of what the visuals show. Here are some dos and don'ts to act on if you want your audience to take on board at a glance what each of your visuals is showing:

- Make sure every visual has a title that indicates what it shows or is about.

- Be sure to label all the elements of a diagram, such as the 'x' and 'y' axes of graphs.

- Use separate visuals for overview and detail. Perhaps you're about to give a presentation made up of four main sections. You may have an 'overview' visual that lists these points. That's fine to use when you're introducing and outlining your presentation, but once you start talking about section 1, it would be a distraction to have all four headings up on the screen. Give each section its own visual.

- Limit the amount of information you put on any one visual; don't include more points or more words than anyone can easily see at a glance or that you can talk about comfortably in, say, one and a half or two minutes.

- Don't 'crowd' the content of your visuals: separating elements by white space makes them much easier to read.

- If your talk is divided into chunks (paragraphs, bullet points or whatever) consider having one visual (but not more than one) to each chunk.

- Make sure your text and any labels can be read by someone at the back of the room. With PowerPoint and OHP transparencies avoid if you can using a typeface (font) with a pitch smaller than 24 points.

- If you're using OHP, PowerPoint or video, make sure that your visuals are not too big for your equipment (e.g. the OHP table or the screen).

- Be consistent in layout, typeface and use of colour. Inconsistencies puzzle and distract your audience.

- If you have material (e.g. two pie charts) that you want your audience to compare, put it on a single visual. You will be making it very difficult for your audience to make the comparison if you're flicking to and fro between a pair of slides, say.

- Beware of using a ready-made, clip-art graphic just because you have it available. Their style is hackneyed, and it's rare that it will make exactly the point you want to make.

## Take special care with continuous slideshows

Nowadays many experienced presenters like to run a 'continuous slide-show'. That is, there is hardly a moment in the presentation when the screen is not filled with some material or other. One reason why they do this is so that the slideshow can be printed off, to provide a ready-made handout of notes for the audience.

If you plan a continuous slideshow you run the risk that you won't properly establish personal communication with your audience, thereby sacrificing the unique benefit of presentation; and it becomes all too easy to make points via the screen when it would be better to make them person to person. You end up showing 'text-heavy' slides, packed with detail. Especially if the slideshow is also to be the handout, you're tempted to pack everything onto the slides. Bear in mind that words are what presenters do best, while visual aids are best for abstractions (such as numerical and spatial relationships) that can be illustrated through diagrams, and for pictures and photographs.

Here's a question. If everything you want to say is on your slides, why are you speaking at all? What do you have to add? Is your presentation going to take the form of you reading your slides to your audience? This is taking accompanying your audience too far. Your audience can read your slides perfectly well for themselves.

Some presenters prepare their presentations by putting everything on slides, then realize that whether they read them out or stay silent it's going to be a pretty embarrassing experience. So they then prepare a commentary to add to the slideshow. Unfortunately this can thoroughly confuse their audience, who are in effect trying to take in two presentations at once: detail-packed slides plus the commentary. So our advice is, don't feel you have to put everything you want to tell your audience on to your slides.

You might like to try turning the screen off between important non-text slides, not by physically switching off the projector but by interposing a 'black slide'. Some recent software includes a 'black screen' command so that you don't even have to put a black slide in the sequence. Or you can achieve this separation by interposing very simple two- or three-word text slides, which break up your presentation like chapter headings in a book. These discreetly remind anyone whose gaze strays to the screen what section of the presentation you're in, but they don't compete with you for your audience's attention, as a diagram, picture or photograph – or a text-heavy slide – would. Muted colours or reduced-intensity lettering will also make it easier for you to take centre stage.

# Handouts

Handouts are usually photo-copies or printouts of salient information given to listeners for them to take away at the end of your presentation.

## The purposes of handouts

You can use a handout to serve some or all of a variety of purposes:

- To reinforce your message. You're not only speaking your message – you're giving it to your listeners in a tangible, take-away form. You're thereby making it more likely that they will absorb it and be able to reproduce it accurately later. So your handout might contain a summary of your reasoning or your conclusions.

- To provide your audience, during your presentation, with the outline of your presentation, to make it easier for them to follow you.

- To save you (and your audience) the chore of reading out or writing or drawing on a board or flipchart reams of factual material, such as quotations, a list of references, diagrams, tables of figures, graphs and pie charts.

- To gain your audience's goodwill. Most people like to have a handout to take away from a presentation, and your forethought in providing one will be appreciated (perhaps irrespective of what it actually contains).

- To provide a record of your slides. If you are using PowerPoint, you will be able to print out your slides – usually six to a side of A4 paper – and give this out as a handout.

## The etiquette of handouts

There are three basic rules that you should follow with regard to handouts:

1.  Decide what purpose(s) your handout is to fulfil and design it accordingly. A direct printout from your PowerPoint slides may not necessarily provide what you require.

2.  Make your handout look good. It should be neat and tidy. Don't cram the pages full of print: leave space between paragraphs, which will make it easier to read and to find things. Don't go crazy with fonts: stick to one (or at most two). Issuing a messy handout shows a lack of respect for your audience.

3.  Take enough for everybody to have one. If this means a few spares, so be it, but make sure you recycle them. (And be aware that some greedy people may grab more than one.) There are few things more frustrating than being in an audience – especially in the middle of a row or at the back – and being pretty sure that at the end there will be a great scramble for handouts, there won't be enough for everyone, and you will miss out.

## When should handouts be handed out?

The answer to this question will depend on the purpose and content of your handout. For example, if it contains all your reasoning and conclusions, you may not want to distribute it until the end of the session. The handout could distract your audience: they could be reading it when you want them to be giving their full attention to you, and you might feel you were 'giving away' your conclusions or 'punchline'.

On the other hand, if the handout contains the outline of your presentation, giving it out at the beginning will help your audience to follow you more easily. If the handout contains tables and/or diagrams, you can lead the audience through these and draw attention to significant features, and your audience know they don't have to copy down such material from slides or whatever. If you follow this model, you might even distribute the handout at the beginning and then allow five minutes for the audience to look through it. Whatever you do, though, don't put so much material on the handout that your audience 'gets it' all during the first five minutes and is then bored while you go through it all again.

# Prompts: index cards, script, notes, annotated printouts

Almost all experienced public speakers make use of some kind of 'prompt'. This can take one of a number of forms: a sequence of index cards, each carrying a message, which the presenter goes through in sequence and uses as reminders of what comes next in the presentation; a script, such as a speech written out in full; notes on particular points, designed to be referred to if necessary; or annotated printouts of slides. You may wish to make use of one or other of these techniques yourself. Here are some things to take into account when deciding which to choose.

## Index cards

Index cards, otherwise known as file cards or record cards, are pieces of card – six inches by four inches (152 mm x 102 mm) is the most popular size – on which you can write key terms or key points that you want to make. Your cards act as 'prompts': they remind you what you want to say, and in what order. You number the cards, to help ensure that they come up, and stay, in the right order, and take them with you when you give your presentation. Many experienced speakers use them.

Index cards are easy to carry and inconspicuous to use. You can take a quick look at a card without losing eye contact with the audience. Rewriting or adding a card is a simple matter.

To use index cards successfully you have to know your subject really well. They are a way of retrieving material from your mind, from your memory; but, for this to happen, you need to have installed it there in the first place. Frankly, you shouldn't even dream of giving a presentation *without* knowing your subject in this way. You should have a clear sense of how the aspects of the subject fit together, and you should be able to explain key points in outline, as if someone had just asked you a question over lunch – even if you then refer to prompts, notes or slides for exact names and numbers. If you're talking on a subject that is quite new to you, you may need to put quite a lot of material on your cards; take care to ensure that every card is legible at a glance.

## Script

In a later section, 'Make your presentation audience-friendly' (pages 87–88), we shall show how useful a script can be in preparing your material for presentation. You should definitely *not* stand in front of your audience and simply read out your script. If you're depending on your script to carry you through your whole presentation, you have not prepared well enough. However, having your script with you when you are actually giving your presentation means that if you lose your train of thought – your 'thread' – you do have your script to refer to. (And you will probably find that your script serves as a kind of 'security blanket'. You will just feel safer.) Once you're back on track, you'll be able to resume a freer way of speaking.

When the time comes to give your presentation, if you need to consult your script you'll want to do so without breaking eye contact with your audience. So you will be positioning the script on the lectern or table, where it takes only a tiny glance down to locate the passage you want. Make this easy for yourself by laying your script out clearly, with headings that leap out at you, with plenty of white space in the margins and between paragraphs, and with a font, pitch and line spacing that are easy on your eyes. And use one side of the paper only, so you don't have to turn pages over.

# Notes

You may have seen people turn up to give presentations carrying a folder of notes through which they then proceed to scrabble while talking somewhat spasmodically to their audience at the same time. You get the (usually accurate) impression that they haven't prepared properly, and that when they're talking to you their mind isn't 100 per cent on the job. The folder may well fulfil the role of a (rather scruffy) security blanket. When you're the presenter, please do your best to avoid giving such an impression.

Yes, there *are* occasions on which you might want to take raw notes with you into a presentation. You might be constructing the presentation around short extracts from half a dozen different documents, for example, and want to have the original documents (or photocopies) with you. Or you might want to be prepared for questions by having every source at your fingertips.

In the former case, it's a good idea to highlight the extracts, so they will be easier to find and read out. It's also a good idea to stick Post-its at the top of the page to act as bookmarks, numbered so you know in which order to take them. You'll be organized, and – no less important – it will be apparent to your audience that you're organized. In the latter case (being prepared for questions) again bookmark the documents but resist any temptation to refer to them while you're giving your presentation.

As a general rule, though, until you've got a lot of experience at thinking on your feet, do your best to avoid having to rely on undigested notes. Do your homework in good time, and either write out your script or prepare a set of index cards.

# Annotated printouts

There is an interesting alternative to script, index cards and notes: the annotated printout. If you are using certain kinds of visual aid – in particular OHP transparencies, photographic slides or PowerPoint slides – you can print these out on to sheets of A4 paper, one film or slide to a sheet. This technique works especially well with PowerPoint slides, since there is a print option of one slide per sheet. The printout of the slide is in the centre of the sheet, and small enough to give wide margins in which you can write notes to accompany the slide.

The beauty of this system is that the slides and your notes are perfectly integrated. When you're creating your presentation, you can design slides and write notes more or less simultaneously. Moreover, with the annotated printout in front of you or in your hand, you don't have to peer at the computer screen or turn round to look at the projected image to see the slide. Do try this technique if you get the opportunity.

\* \* \*

Whatever kind of prompt you're using, it is important to be able to use it without breaking eye contact with your audience for longer than is absolutely necessary. Ideally, you will be able to look at it and take in at a glance the words, symbols and/or pictures on it. For an exercise that will help you to do this, see Exercise 15, 'Rehearsing using prompts', on pages 102–3.

# Team presentations

## Creating a joint presentation

We made the point earlier that any academic process that involves working with words comprises three strands: doing your homework, thinking about your topic, and deciding your plan. If several of you are going to be working on a project and are to give a presentation on it when you have finished, you do need to bear the presentation stage in mind from the very beginning. It is all too common, when a group of students are assigned a project, for them to divide the work up among themselves and each go off and do his or her own thing. When they get together just before giving their presentation they find that they've been working on different assumptions and interpretations of the brief, that they have incompatible ideas about the solution to the problem posed, and that gaps and overlaps in their work as a whole are evident. Typically, when each person has dealt with one aspect of the project, the audience finds that in the presentation one or two use Power-Point, another uses an OHP, and yet another just talks. The lack of organization of the presentation reveals the lack of organization of the work that has preceded it.

Accordingly the first requirement for producing a team presentation is that you work together jointly, as a team, on your project. You may not find this easy – after all, the ethos of the education system is one of individual achievement – but it is worth making the effort (you can get some help from one of the other books in the Student-Friendly Guides series, *Successful Teamwork!*). Your team could decide to appoint one of you to coordinate the presentation, so that at the very least there is a common format for visual aids and a single handout. This person needs to have substantive work to do on the project too, if he or she is not to get very frustrated waiting for the others to produce work. But if the presentation coordinator continually keeps an eye out for any tendency for people to work in isolation and pulls them back into the team, he or she will be performing a very valuable function.

## Planning introductions, handovers and conclusion

It will pay you to give some thought at the preparation stage to how your team members will be introduced, how you will manage the handover as one member ends his or her part of the presentation and hands over to the next, and how you will end the presentation.

You will need to decide, for example, whether one member – and, if so, who – will introduce the other members and himself or herself; you may consider that this is preferable to having each member introducing themselves.

And it will help to have a particular form of words to use when handing over to the next presenter, perhaps something along the lines of: 'In this part of our presentation I have shown how we formulated the problem. I'm now going to hand over to my colleague, X, who will demonstrate the range of alternative solutions that we considered.' You are performing together, like actors who have to know each other's cues.

Finally, it would be worthwhile deciding in advance whether your presentation as a whole will simply come to an end when the last presenter stops talking, or whether one of you will provide a brief summary by way of rounding off your presentation. That might be a very satisfying thing to do.

# Part Four

# Thinking about your audience

# Make your presentation audience-friendly

Having assembled your material, decided your plan and adjusted it to make your message memorable, you've got your first draft. Your next task is to make your draft and your whole presentation audience-friendly.

We suggest that, especially if you're just starting out on your presentation career, you think of your draft as the 'script' for your presentation. This is *not* so you have something to read out word for word to your audience – that's a thoroughly bad idea – but because when you have typed out your script there are several valuable things you can do with it. In particular, you can redraft it to make it more conversational, more audience-friendly. Read it aloud slowly to yourself, and simplify it wherever possible. Here are some basic rules to follow:

1. Keep your sentences simple. Break up long and/or complex

sentences into short, straightforward ones.

2. Perhaps you've been planning to use words or expressions that not everyone in your audience will be familiar with: it is better to use simpler language, or to include definitions of tricky or unusual terms. (If they hear a word that sets them off thinking 'What does that mean?', they become distracted and you will have lost them.)

3. You can drop the formal language of 'academicspeak'. For example, rather than saying 'It was calculated that ...' you can say 'I worked out that ...'.

4. Use numbered lists and brief repetition wherever you can. For example, 'There are three things to notice. First, ... The second thing to notice is ... The third thing to notice is ...'.

Once you have redrafted your script to make it more conversational, more audience-friendly, read it aloud again and, as you do so, imagine that you are talking to some of your friends. As you read it, highlight or underline the words, phrases or sentences that you are emphasizing, and insert marks to show where you are pausing.

# Make friends with your audience

Giving a presentation will be a much less nerve-racking business if you feel that your audience are friendly towards you: well-disposed, not hostile. Making your actual presentation as audience-friendly as possible, along the lines set out in the last section (pages 87–88), and making good use of visual aids and handouts (see pages 64–76), are all good ways of earning your audience's goodwill and thereby engendering friendliness towards you.

There are several other things you can do to earn your audience's goodwill. Make sure everyone can hear you and can see the whiteboard, flipchart or screen that you'll be using: 'Can I just do a quick sound and sight check?' This is not only a practical thing to do, and not just a matter of putting your audience at their ease – you are also giving them the message that you *care* whether they can hear and see you comfortably.

## Communicating through body language and eye contact

When you are giving a presentation, you are communicating with your audience not only through the words you speak and the visuals you show, but also through the movements of your body and through looking into your audience's eyes while they look into yours. In other words, you also communicate through your body language and through mutual eye contact. Indeed, not only do you yourself generate body language and eye contact, you elicit them from your listeners. And the more committed you are to communicating your message, the more 'positive' the body language and eye contact you generate and – almost always – the more you elicit from your listeners in return.

Similarly, the more energy (of whatever kind: see pages 24–29) you are putting in to your presentation, the more positive the body language and eye contact that you generate and elicit.

For example, if you stand in front of your audience with your arms folded or held stiffly by your sides, and direct your eyes alternately to your notes and the ceiling, people in your audience are likely to slump in their seats and not look at you. If, however, you are using your hands to emphasize the points you are making, and offering eye contact to your audience, they are more likely to take on a more alert posture and respond to your eyes with their own. You are also more likely to feel you are among friends. It's a virtuous – as opposed to a vicious – circle.

Get in the habit of smiling! Look at your audience and smile at everyone who is smiling at you. Then look around and smile at everyone else. Do this at the beginning and take advantage of every smile directed towards you to respond.

Eye contact, together with body language in the form of facial expression, sends an unspoken message. For example, when you are speaking and someone else is listening, the look in your eyes and on your face will be asking non-verbally 'Have you understood?' and the look in your listener's eyes, and on his or her face, will be saying non-verbally 'Go on, this is really interesting' or 'Hang on! You've lost me.'

It is not at all necessary that eye contact be sustained for a length of time. Sometimes just a glance is sufficient to provide a feeling of connection and 'rapport'. During a spoken question-and-answer session you and the questioner may well hold each other's gaze, but if you need to take time out to think you'll probably look away while you're doing your thinking.

To end this section, some words of warning. As a presenter, if you are at all alert to your audience you will notice whether their eyes are upon you, and you will register their body language too. It is very easy to jump to wrong conclusions from what you observe. You may see your 9 am audience sitting slumped in their chairs and conclude that this is a really unfriendly crowd and you're boring them stiff, whereas in fact they were partying until the early hours and are sensationally hungover, and it is a compliment to you that they've showed up at all at 9 am. Likewise, you may see your audience's eyes turned downwards instead of looking at you and conclude that you are being deeply uninteresting, whereas they are in fact concentrating on writing down your every word and are far from being uninterested. Watch those pens! If most people are writing furiously, pause in your presentation until they've slowed or stopped, at which point they'll probably look up at you expectantly.

Never forget that people listen with their ears, not their eyes. So be prepared for audience reaction that on the face of it seems to be unsupportive. Yes, you aim to communicate to individual members of the audience, but don't get discouraged if you look at someone and they look away or even blank you. Look at someone else: you'll usually find fairly quickly the feedback that gives you 'permission to continue'. Only if such feedback consistently eludes you would it be sensible to draw the inference that they're not 'getting it', and look for different words to make your point.

# Speak with authority

As a student, you are unlikely – unless you are coming to the end of your PhD studies – to be an authority on the subject on which you are presenting. So don't attempt to imitate your lecturers when you give a presentation – be yourself, a learner. That does not mean, however, that you will be speaking with no authority. You acquire authority – and respect – by following these rules:

- Show that you have done your homework. If you have done the required reading and other preparation, and put some thought into it, make this evident in your presentation, including your handouts and visuals.

- Be organized. A well-organized presentation indicates a systematic, thoughtful mind at work, and commands respect.

- Cite your sources. You can 'borrow' authority from the authoritative sources you have encountered: 'According to X, ...'. But don't cite X without having read and understood what he or she has written: it is highly likely that you will be found out. Being exposed as a 'name-dropper' does *not* enhance your authority.

● Exercise care in making judgements. A presentation peppered with 'I think' will not command respect. Academic work requires you to marshal relevant evidence and draw reasoned conclusions from it, not spout off with your own opinions.

● Tell your story. We suggested earlier (pages 58–59) that you could make the subject of your presentation the story of how you tackled your topic: how you interpreted the topic, how you worked out what material you needed and/or what sources you had to consult, how you reasoned your way to your conclusion, what problems you encountered en route, what issues your exploration, investigation or review raised for you. There's no harm in saying it again – this approach does free you from the temptation to pretend that you're an authority on the subject. You can be yourself: a student, a person striving to learn.

Doing all these things successfully will impress both your teachers and your fellow learners, and they will be keenly interested in what you have to say.

# Conquer your nerves

Just about everyone, even experienced presenters, feels nervous before giving a presentation. A touch of nerves is by no means a bad thing. When you're about to begin your presentation they generate the hormone adrenalin, which will give you energy and keep you 'on your toes', and your presentation will be all the better for it. But if you're contemplating a presentation that you're due to give some days or weeks in the future and you get a sinking feeling in your stomach and can't eat or get to sleep at night, your nerves aren't helping you. What can you do about them?

Nerves have a number of sources. In part they come about through worrying – you think about all the things that could go wrong. This is your head at work. You're consciously anticipating a disaster scenario: in your mind you can see, hear and feel all the elements of a disaster coming together.

Nerves also come about without engaging in any conscious thought processes. They bypass your head altogether. They just hit you – in your mouth, your throat or the pit of your stomach. Perhaps some traumatic moment from your childhood, buried in your subconscious, has been resurrected: your first day at school, perhaps, or an occasion when you were humiliated by a teacher.

Fortunately there are many things you can do to bring your nerves under control. Here we offer four suggestions:

1.  appreciating the work you've done
2.  avoiding negative self-labelling
3.  visualizing success
4.  thinking differently about giving your presentation.

Essentially they are mental exercises. They require nothing by way of equipment, only a quiet place where you can be on your own, and they require you to disclose nothing about yourself to other people. All are perfectly do-able, tried and tested and found to work.

### Exercise 11: Appreciating the work you've done

*Purpose*
This is a great exercise to boost your confidence.

*Equipment*
None.

*What you do*
Collect together your prompts and all the other material you've prepared, including handouts and visuals. Look at the sheer quantity of what you have in front of you. It is your safety net: it will protect you from falling to earth with a thump. Compare what you know about your topic now with what you knew when you started out: this will remind you how far you've progressed and how much you now have 'under your belt'.

### Exercise 12: Avoiding negative self-labelling

*Purpose*
To open your mind to the idea that you can be comfortable when you are the centre of attention.

Being a presenter involves being the centre of attention. You may not be accustomed to this and may feel uncomfortable about it. Maybe you feel self-conscious when the spotlight is on you. Perhaps you see yourself as a modest, self-effacing, limelight-shunning sort of person – a dependable supporter of others, maybe, rather than a pushy, attention-grabbing loudmouth.

The problem with labelling yourself in this way is that it becomes a self-fulfilling prophecy. The more you tell yourself that you are a 'happiest in the background' sort of person, the more you are closing your mind to strategies that would help you to be comfortable occupying a place in the foreground.

*Equipment*
None.

*What you do*
Take a minute or two to think back to a situation where you have been with other people and have felt comfortable and relaxed with them, able to be yourself, joining in the conversation and being listened to when you do. Picture the scene in your mind's eye: the room, the furniture, the company, and so on. Hear again the conversation, yourself and the others speaking. Recapture your feelings: the warmth you felt, your pleasure, your enjoyment, the sense of being appreciated and valued. Smile to yourself as you see that scene again, hear those sounds again, feel those pleasurable feelings again. Make a habit of doing this, with other past situations too, and you'll find yourself switching from negative to positive self-labelling.

**Exercise 13: Visualizing success**

*Purpose*
To open your mind to the possibility that your presentation will be a great success.

Prophecies, like labels, are often self-fulfilling. If you anticipate problems, you will certainly have problems. You'll be on the lookout for them, you'll tune in to them, they'll jump out at you. If an athlete started a race with his or her mind focused on 'problems', it would not be conducive to winning. It's the same for you. So, anticipate success instead. Then it'll be ways of achieving success that spring to your attention.

*Equipment*
None.

*What you do*
Visualize success! If you can, go and take a look at the room that you'll be presenting in. Then, in your mind's eye, run a movie of yourself standing in that room giving your presentation. See, hear and feel yourself talking confidently, pointing out features on your visuals and distributing your handouts. Your behaviour will live up to the image that you have of yourself. That's how it works.

**Exercise 14: Thinking differently about giving your presentation**

*Purpose*
If you instinctively view giving a presentation as an ordeal, this exercise will help you to view it in a more positive light.

*Equipment*
None.

*What you do*
Brainstorm! Think about the opportunity that preparing and giving a

presentation affords you. It could be an opportunity to explore a subject, pose some interesting questions about it, trigger off a discussion and get some valuable feedback from other people. So you're an explorer and a thought-provoker.

Or it could be an opportunity to play with the puzzle that your topic poses: to highlight discrepancies in the literature you have read, to test hypotheses and generalizations, to try out theories, and so on. This time you're an intellectual gymnast.

Choose what *you* would like to be.

For more exercises along these lines, see *Sail through exams!,* a companion volume in the Student-Friendly Guides series.

# Part Five

# Rehearse!
## Rehearse!
### Rehearse!

# The benefits of rehearsing

## How rehearsing helps

To give a really good presentation you *must* rehearse it. Even experienced presenters rehearse carefully. Very few 'wing it', although they may make it look spontaneous and effortless when they perform. Giving a good presentation is a very physical activity, and you should no more think of doing it without rehearsing than you would playing competitive sport or going dancing.

Crucially, rehearsing will help you to give your presentation without having to think self-consciously about what you're doing while you're doing it. It helps you to 'internalize' it, so you don't have to ask yourself consciously what comes next – if you have rehearsed it properly it will come to your mind automatically, like the next line of a poem that you know well. So rehearsing will free your mind during the actual presentation to concentrate on the immediate moment. Your mind won't be on other things, like what you're going to say next or whether you have time to get everything in. (Audiences always notice such distraction, and respond negatively to it.)

So when you're just starting, take every opportunity to rehearse, wherever you are: in your room (in front of the mirror is a good place), in an empty office, or even on a walk in the countryside. But because presentation is *above all* for your audience, it's a great help if you can get a friend or a sympathetic fellow student to join you when you're rehearsing. Just practising talking about the subject to your friends will fix your sequence of points in your mind. If you are giving a presentation in a language other than your own mother tongue, a native speaker of that language is a very good person to have around.

Rehearsing will also help you to get your timing right. It is a common failing of presenters, even experienced ones, that they try to cram in more material than they have time for. So they end up talking too fast – even gabbling – or leaving out important points. Our advice, then, is to rehearse your presentation in full, talking at presentation speed, as many times as it is necessary for you to be sure that you are familiar with your material and that it fits your allotted time.

# Rehearse using your prompts

In the section entitled 'Make your presentation audience-friendly' (pages 87–88), we suggested that you prepare a draft of your presentation, and that you go through it altering it to make it more conversational and audience-friendly, and marking it up to show emphases and pauses. We also suggested that you read it aloud while imagining that you are talking to some of your friends. This is the basis for a useful rehearsal exercise, Exercise 15: 'Rehearsing using prompts'.

### Exercise 15: Rehearsing using prompts

*Purpose*

This is a simulation exercise to give you a 'dry run' rehearsal of your presentation.

*Equipment*
A private, quiet room and one or more friends, if possible in person rather than in your imagination. Your script and a pen.

*What you do*
Holding your script in front of you, read the first sentence silently to yourself. Then you put your script down and, without looking at it, speak that sentence to your friends. When you're satisfied that you are communicating strongly with your audience, do the same with the next sentence, and so on. You'll probably want to amend your emphases and pauses, and maybe slow your rate of speaking. You might like to stop every now and again to ask your friends if they have any (constructive) comments.

Once you are happy with your delivery, read your script aloud once more and time yourself while you do so. (You don't need your friends to be present for this.) You may find that you have to make cuts in order to keep within the time allowed you.

All this reading and rereading of your script may strike you as repetitious and tedious. Leave some time, and do other things, between readings, so you come to each with a reasonably fresh mind. There will almost certainly come a point at which (a) you can find nothing that you feel you need to improve, and (b) when you turn over a page and see the one underneath, you have a warm feeling of recognition. This is a very good feeling to have. You are beginning to associate your presentation with comfort and familiarity. Much better than associating it with fear and anxiety.

# Using your visual aids

There are two important practical skills that you need when using your visual aids: using a pointer and shifting the audience's attention to and fro between you and your visual. Here are two rehearsal exercises that will help you to master them.

## Using a pointer

Exercise 16 – 'Using a stick or laser pen with a visual on a screen' – is a practical rehearsal exercise to help you to be comfortable with whatever method of pointing you are going to use for your presentation.

### Exercise 16: Using a stick or laser pen with a visual on a screen

*Purpose*
This is a simple exercise to accustom you to using a stick or laser pen in a way that comes easily to you (so you don't have to think about it when you're doing it) and that doesn't lead to you blocking someone's view. It provides you with a 'good practice' checklist.

*Equipment*
You'll need to be in the room that you're going to use for your presentation, or one very like it, and provided with the same visual aid and pointer that you will be using for the actual event. You'll also need to have your visuals with you, of course.

*What you do*
Put one of your visuals up on the screen.

1.  Take the pointer in your hand and point to something on the screen. Hold it right there! Stand still and look over your shoulder towards the seats where your audience will be sitting. *Check*: Would anyone in the audience have their view blocked? If so, adjust your position to give as many people as possible a clear view.

2.  *Check*: Which arm are you using? Are you using the arm that's closer to the audience? If so, you may be muffling your voice. Change arms so you're using the one nearer the screen.

3.  *Check*: Are you as close as possible to the plane of the screen? If not, move so that you *are* as close to it as possible. That way, the visual will be visible to almost everybody in your audience. However, you will now be standing at a very oblique angle to the screen; take the opportunity to get used to viewing your visuals from that angle.

4.  *Check*: Are you moving about while you are pointing to your visual? If so, you are likely to be distracting your audience – they will be looking at you when you want them to be looking at your visual. Try to keep still while using your pointer.

5.  *Check*: Is there more you can do to draw your audience's attention to

the element of your visual that you are pointing to? Try saying things like 'Over here, on the left, you can see . . .'.

# Shifting the audience's attention between you and your visual

During your presentation, there will be times when you want your audience's attention to be on your visual, and times when you want it to be on *you*. (Don't leave it to your visuals to do all the work.) Shifting their attention to and fro is a valuable skill, and one that needs to be developed during your rehearsal. Exercise 17 will help you to do this.

### Exercise 17: Shifting the audience's attention between you and your visual

*Purpose*
This is an exercise to help you to master simple techniques for shifting your audience's attention between yourself and the visual that you are showing.

*Equipment*
As for Exercise 16, you'll need to be in the room that you're going to use for your presentation, or one very like it, and provided with the same visual aid and pointer that you will be using for the actual event. You'll also need to have your visuals with you, of course.

*What you do*
Put one of your visuals up on the screen.

To direct your audience's attention to your visual, make a definite turn towards it. Move your feet, so you turn your body and your head, and look at your visual, up on the screen. Your audience will look where you are looking. Don't spoil the effect by immediately turning back to face them. Instead, maintain your connection to your audience *through* the visual. Imagine you are sending out your voice, with your message, to them *via* the screen. You may need to speak a little louder to do this effectively. Practise doing this.

When you have finished with that visual, you will want to get the audience's attention back onto yourself. There are three ways you can do this:

1. Experiment to find a comfortable way of switching the visual off. If you are using an OHP turn it off or remove the transparency. If you are using PowerPoint, move to a 'black screen' or blank slide. (If you leave the visual showing, it will simply compete with you for attention.)

2. Step up your energy level. Speak a little louder, or with more emphasis, or ask a question. Make eye contact with your audience.

3. Take a step towards your audience. People are conditioned to react very strongly to such movements.

Practise all these actions, using different visuals, until you can perform them naturally.

# Working as a team

Team members have a vital function even while they are not speaking. They can make the speaker look good, or they can sabotage the speaker's efforts.

Actors know this well. If you are playing the part of the Queen, for instance, it is the attitude of your courtiers that confers royal status on you. If they are all paying attention to you, and move and talk only in response to you, you look important. If they are fidgeting or talking among themselves, you look unimportant.

When taking part in a team presentation, if you are speaking and your team is in view of the audience, they will help you enormously if they pay attention to you. If your audience's eyes wander towards your colleagues, when they see that your colleagues' eyes are focused on you their own eyes will return to you.

However, it is not easy for the non-speaking team members to be attentive to the speaker. If you have yet to speak, you may be preoccupied with what you are going to say and unable to resist looking through your notes. If you've had your turn, your senses may be swamped by your feelings of relief.

So discipline within teams needs to be practised. Exercise 18 – 'Team presentations: practising discipline' – offers a simple way of doing this and at the same time rehearsing for your presentation.

### Exercise 18: Team presentations: practising discipline

*Purpose*
This is a role-play and simulation exercise to sensitize you to the need to pay attention to the team member who is speaking.

*Equipment*
A private, quiet room. All the members of your team should be present.

*What you do*
There are three roles: one speaker, one observer and as many colleagues as there are others of you. You will take turns at being speaker and observer and there will be three rounds (i.e. you will each have three goes at those two roles). If there are only two of you in your team, the roles of speaker and observer will have to be combined.

The *first round* begins. The first speaker speaks for three minutes (timed by the observer), as if to a real audience. The colleagues behave as they would normally. The observer watches for what appears to be unhelpful behaviour on the part of the colleagues and makes a note of it. At the end of the three minutes there is a pause while the speaker makes a note of any behaviour by colleagues that he or she found off-putting or unhelpful. Then do the exercise again with a new speaker and observer, and repeat until everyone has had a turn at both roles. You now review the first round, each 'active' pair (speaker and observer) offering their notes and colleagues listening. Note that listening is all you do: you should not argue or attempt to justify your behaviour.

The *second round* now begins. The procedure is the same as for the first round, except that this time the colleagues are expected to modify their behaviour to take account of the points made by the observer and speaker in the first round. In reviewing the second round, you say if you feel there has been any improvement on the first, and whether further improvement would be possible.

The *third round* follows the pattern of the second. By now you should see a definite improvement compared with the first round.

If colleagues find it quite impossible to give the speaker their full attention, it might be best to position them out of view of the audience. One option is to put them in the front row of the audience, ready to come on to speak. However, in those seats they would be in full view of the speaker and might constitute a considerable distraction to him or her. An alternative would be to place them to one side. But these are very much second-best solutions. When someone else is speaking, please do your best to give them your full attention.

# Handovers

Handovers should always be rehearsed. A poor handover is like dropping the baton in a relay race: you lose momentum and dissipate energy, and the next speaker has to work really hard to generate them again.

In the section entitled 'Team presentations' (pages 81–83), we noted the need to have a form of words to use when handing over to the next presenter, and gave an example. Formulate those that will be appropriate for your particular presentation. Exercise 19 – 'Team presentations: practising handovers' – will give you actions that go along with the words.

### Exercise 19: Team presentations: practising handovers

*Purpose*
This is an exercise to help you make smooth handovers when giving a team presentation.

*Equipment*
A private, quiet room. Ideally all members of your team will be present. You need a piece of paper on which each of you apart from the last speaker has written down your summary/introduction line. This will be along the lines of 'In this part of our presentation I have shown how we formulated the problem. I'm now going to hand over to my colleague, Charles, who will demonstrate the range of alternative solutions that we considered.'

*What you do*
You are performing a chain of handovers. At any time the members of your team who are not currently engaged in the presentation will constitute the audience. If there are only two of you, designate a chair or table to represent your audience. There will be two rounds (i.e. you go through the chain twice).

As first speaker, hold the piece of paper with the summary/introduction lines and – facing your audience – speak your particular line. As you say the words 'my colleague, Charles', make eye contact with Charles, and hold that eye contact while he gets up and comes towards you. As you finish your line, hold the piece of paper out to him. Charles takes the paper, says 'Thank you' to you, and then turns to make eye contact with the audience before starting his line.

In this physical handover, you will almost certainly find that you naturally hold eye contact with Charles until he signals (with his eyes) that he has got hold of the paper. You yourself will automatically be looking not at the paper but at his eyes. And it will be only when Charles turns away to make eye contact with the audience that you are 'released' to fade away into the background. The round continues until the last speaker has received the piece of paper.

In the second round, you follow the same procedure but without the piece of paper. With no physical handover, there may be a greater physical distance between you and Charles, but the stages of eye contact will be the same. First, it will be between you and your audience; then between you and Charles, until he signals that he has 'received' the handover and thanks you; then between Charles and the audience.

You may like to repeat the second round until all of you are comfortable with it.

# Part Six

# Last-minute checks

# Check out the room

If at all possible, check out the room in which you will be giving your presentation. Pay attention to the space, to lighting and visibility, and to seating. Test it in the following ways. This should take only a few minutes and it will be time well spent.

## Space

- Find your 'home position', the position you need to be in to be able to see your notes or script and have all controls at your fingertips. So this position might be close to the desk, lectern, microphone, whiteboard, OHP, or to a computer that operates a projector. Once you have found your home position, how much room for manoeuvre have you got? Pay special attention to movement towards the audience and back. Is there a

**115**

lectern? Is it set at, or close enough to, the correct height for you? Do you have to use it? Be aware that if you stand behind a desk or lectern the audience may feel there is a barrier between you and them.

● Notice which seat or seats are the furthest from you. You will need to speak loudly and energetically enough for people sitting in those seats to be able to hear you.

● Check whether you can see all the seats from your home position and any other position that you might move into. If there are seats you can't see, people sitting in them won't be able to see you. It will be sensible to avoid placing yourself where you can't be seen.

## Lighting and visibility

● Check whether your home position and any other position into which you might move is well lit. A presenter whose features can clearly be seen will make more of an impression on the audience than one in the shadows. If your home position is not well lit, do everything you can to improve the lighting, or move.

● Beware of any position in which members of the audience would see you against the background of an uncovered window. The light behind you will display your silhouette nicely but make it hard for them to see your features. If this might be a problem, see if you can pull a blind or draw a curtain over the window.

## Seating

Check whether the seating is arranged as you want it. If not, are you able to change it? You may want:

● desks at which people can write

● easy chairs rather than upright chairs, to encourage a relaxed, informal atmosphere, or vice versa, to encourage a businesslike atmosphere

● seats arranged in a circle: this configuration encourages discussion, as everyone can see everyone else. Make sure that the circle will be large enough to accommodate everyone: somebody seated outside the circle may feel inhibited from taking part

- certain areas blocked off: if you find yourself in a room designed for lectures, with seats in rows facing you, and if your audience will be appreciably smaller than the capacity of the room, you might like to rope off areas so they don't leave the front row empty, or to group them in the centre so you don't have to behave like a tennis umpire to make eye contact with everyone.

Incidentally, checking out the room can be a good way of calming your nerves. Your attention is directed outwards, to the environment in which you will be presenting, rather than inwards, to any tensions that you may be feeling.

# Check out the equipment

Locate the equipment you will be using. Check the position of the screen, whiteboard or flipchart. Will they be visible to everyone in your audience? Find the pointer you'll be using, and practise using it. Use the checklist in Exercise 16 (pages 105–6) to make sure you do so effectively.

Find the controls for the electrical and/or electronic equipment you'll be using. Are they near your home position? Check how much walking about you'll have to do, and that there are no cables on the floor that you might trip over.

Make sure that electrical and/or electronic aids work.

- If you are using an OHP, switch it on, check that it works and is correctly focused and will show the entire area of your biggest diagram. Make sure that your transparencies are in the correct order, with sheets of white tissue paper interleaved between them so they are easy to manipulate.

● If you are using PowerPoint, switch on the computer and projector. (You may first have to find out how to do this.) Log on. Load your file and get your first slide up on the screen. Check that you are happy with it. Check that the controls behave in the way that you expect.

● If you are using a whiteboard or flipchart, make sure you have the correct marker pens. (You *must* use 'dry-wipe' markers on a whiteboard – permanent markers will ruin it and you will be highly embarrassed when you try to erase the marks.) If markers are supplied, make sure they haven't dried up and that there is the range of colours you want. Experienced presenters bring their own markers.

● If you will be using a microphone, make sure you know where the controls are and that it is correctly set up. Ideally it won't tether you to a single spot on the floor. But do consider whether you really need it: a real, live voice is always better, provided you can make yourself heard without strain.

Finally, check that you have all your personal gear with you: your prompts, OHP transparencies if you're using them, your PowerPoint presentation on a floppy disk or other portable storage device (with any connector required) and preferably backed up on another. If you're taking in a bottle of water, a nice glass to drink from will add a pleasing professional touch.

# Part Seven

Giving your
presentation

# Away you go...

If you have worked your way through the exercises in this book, you will be well on the way to developing good habits, and many dos and don'ts will already be becoming second nature to you. This section is designed for light last-minute reading before a presentation, just to remind you of some of the most important ones and offer you a few final tips.

## Meeting your audience

When you meet your audience, or as they assemble after you've already entered the room, it is just possible that you might get an unpleasant surprise. Somebody with whom you're having a fierce argument may have turned up, there may be a message from your teacher saying he's had to go to a conference and forgot to cancel the session but please carry on without him, or there may be far fewer people present than you anticipated. Just remember this: *you have a job to do!* You have prepared for it, by doing your homework, thinking about the topic and working on your presentation skills, so concentrate your thoughts on doing it to the best of your ability. Even if only one person has turned up to listen to you, that person deserves your full attention. Ignore those who aren't there. Put the sole attender at his or her ease ('How nice to see you!') and show you can carry off what might otherwise have been an embarrassing situation.

Regrettably, it will not be unusual if some people turn up after you've started. Latecomers often create disruption and distraction for those already in the room. You may want to pause for a moment while they get settled, and then carry on ('As I was saying, . . .'). Your first loyalty should be to those who did you the courtesy of turning up on time.

## Starting your presentation

There are two things you should do before you start to speak. Take deep breaths (breathe out fully before each one, this will ensure that you then breathe in deeply too) and tense some of your muscles, then release the tension. Remember the exercises you've done.

If someone else is taking the chair for you, it will be their task to create a silence and invite you to start. If no one introduces you or calls for silence, and your audience are chatting among themselves while waiting for you to start, what can you do to attract their attention, so they fall silent and look at you? The answer is to speak loudly, with energy in your voice. Take a deep breath and let your voice come out loudly enough to sound commanding. With practice you'll find it easy to gauge this. For a novice, it's probably better to overdo it than underdo it: you avoid sounding as though you're pleading with your audience to let you speak, and you can lower your voice once you have their attention. If you stand up, that will help to get your audience's attention, but do this only if it's appropriate.

Some presenters like to attract their audience's attention by tapping on the table. If you want to do this, make sure your taps are really loud and distinct. Tapping, however, does nothing to open your lungs and airways, so do put on your most commanding voice. It's usually fine to say something innocuous, like 'Welcome to this seminar', 'Now that we're all here, ...', 'Let's make a start!' or 'Today's topic is ...'.

## Once you've got going ...

As well as bringing vocal energy to the proceedings, try to bring other forms of energy too. Make appropriate gestures with your hands. Let your eyes and the expression on your face convey energy. If you are beginning by saying something arresting, don't say it in a 'deadpan' way – put *feeling* into it. Use pauses for effect. If you ask a question, pause for a few seconds after it, not only to give your audience time to digest it but also to create some tension, while your audience wonder what the answer will be or indeed whether you are going to tell them the answer. If you're telling a story, make a drama out of it.

Find friendly faces to talk to. Your audience give you the energy you need to keep going. Try smiling! Look at your audience and smile at everyone who is smiling at you. Then look around and smile at everyone else. Do this at the beginning and take advantage of every smile directed towards you to respond.

Use confident body language and make eye contact confidently, and you will *feel* confident. That's how it works!

There will be points during your presentation at which you want to change the energy level in the room, to 'cool it', then re-energize it. To do this, when – for example – you get to the end of one section and are about to start another, you could say: 'So, what I've established is this: ... Are there any questions so far?' and then, after dealing with questions, 'Good! Let me continue' or 'Right! Let's carry on.'

Please remember the point we made earlier: you aren't 'delivering' your presentation in a take-it-or-leave-it way, merely uttering the words and leaving it to your audience to do what they want with it. Instead you're actively *giving* it to your listeners. Think of yourself as 'handing it over', as you would a gift, with appropriate gestures, facial expression and of course eye contact. All of these will convey energy in a way that mere 'delivery' doesn't.

It is crucially important that you be audible to everyone in your audience. Every now and again, while you're speaking, turn to the person(s) furthest away from you. Make eye contact if possible. If they can't hear you clearly, you will immediately find this out. Making eye contact with your audience will also help you to gauge that your point is getting across. This should help you not to speak too quickly, which will in turn give you time to articulate your words clearly. And please don't hold your hand or notes in front of your mouth.

If people in your audience will want or need to copy down material on your visuals, please give them time to do so. If you watch their hands, you will see when they are ready to listen to you again. Bear in mind the problem that they have if you are commenting on a slide. If you want them to copy down what's on the slide *and* to listen to what you are saying and write *that* down, you must allow them the time to do this. So watch your audience's hands. Try not to continue your presentation until their hands are still. And never remove a slide until they have finished copying from it.

# Question-and-answer sessions

There are many skilled presenters who dread question-and-answer sessions. They may fear the audience will be aggressive; they may worry about not having control of the situation; or they may be afraid of getting a question that they won't be able to answer and of looking stupid as a result.

Aggression from a questioner is sometimes encountered, but it's rare. Your audience will be far more interested in your message than in you, the messenger; and people will ask questions because they want to make sure they've understood, or because they're interested in learning more about what you've told them. The rest of the audience will usually be embarrassed by a questioner's rudeness or bad behaviour: if you keep cool, they'll be on your side.

It is of course true that in question-and-answer sessions you have much less control than you do while you're presenting. Members of the audience are setting the agenda and contributing their energy, which may fizz about all over the place. You need a strategy for dealing with this situation.

Similarly, if you *do* get a question that you won't be able to answer, you need a strategy for dealing with this situation too.

# Managing the session

How a question-and-answer session is managed will depend on who is doing the managing. If you, the presenter, are in charge you will have more scope for managing than if there is a chairperson, a 'chair', especially if the chair is someone in a position of authority, such as your teacher.

If you are in charge, there are several useful management strategies you can adopt. You can:

- manage the opening of the session
- take on the role of communication 'hub'
- reiterate and elucidate questions
- keep cool in the face of difficult questions
- take the sting out of aggressive questions.

## Manage the opening of the session

Here are a couple of things you can do.

- You can acknowledge that you have reached a point where you are sharing control with your audience, by visibly lowering your energy level: take a step back from the audience, take a sip of water from your glass, allow yourself a moment of silence.

- You can offer a starting point for questions: 'Are there any matters of fact, or to do with my sources, that you'd like clarified?' It's better to get these matters out of the way before going on to questions of your methodology or conclusions.

## Take on the role of communication 'hub'

It will help you to keep the session moderately under control if you can become the centre of communication. To do this:

- if a number of hands go up, choose whose question to take, in which order: this establishes you as the central person in the room
- invite questions to yourself and direct your answer to the questioner: this too marks you out as the central person
- if it happens that members of your audience start talking to one another, you could look at them and ask 'Can I help?': you'll be reinforcing your central role. If they're talking about your presentation, you may well be able to help; if they aren't, turning the spotlight on them will probably quieten them.

## Reiterate and elucidate questions

This can be a very useful management technique, because – like the others – it establishes you as the person in charge. Reiterating (repeating) the question is not only a way of making sure that everyone else besides you and the questioner can hear it; it also gives you a moment to 'digest' the question and formulate your answer, and it gives you the opportunity to elucidate the question: 'I'm not altogether clear what you're driving at ... Do you mean ...?'

## Keep cool in the face of difficult questions

It is all too easy to get flustered if someone puts to you a question that you can't answer, and looking and acting flustered (a) are not the marks of a good manager, and (b) will embarrass the audience. If you do get such a question, do remember the basis of your authority (see pages 92–93): you are not the expert on the subject, Mr or Ms Knowall, and you should not be pretending to be. You have, we hope, done your homework, given a reasonably well-organized presentation, cited your sources, exercised care in making judgments, and told your story. You are a *student*, a person striving to learn. There is no shame in not knowing the answer to every question. If the question raises a point you hadn't thought of before, or tells you something you didn't already know, thank the questioner and be pleased that your presentation has led to *you* – not just your audience – learning something.

## Take the sting out of aggressive questions

Aggressive questions are like firecrackers: they come packed with energy (they can certainly raise the temperature!), and are delivered with intent to shock. The questioner may be trying to demonstrate his or her superiority, or may simply be hostile to your ideas. Whichever, try not to take their behaviour as being directed towards you personally.

There are three things you can do with a firecracker: hand it back, promptly; defuse it; or kick it out of the room.

1. *Hand it back, promptly.* You might answer the question with one of your own: 'On what evidence do you base your view?' Or, if you can spot a flawed assumption behind the question, 'You are assuming that X is the case. The evidence does not support this.' Or, if it's an opinion that is being expressed, 'You are, of course, entitled to your opinion. And I am entitled to mine, which – as you can see – is different.'

2. *Defuse it.* You do this by taking the question at face value, ignoring its aggressive overtones and reformulating it if necessary, and answering it to the best of your ability. This deprives the firecracker of its explosive quality.

3. *Kick it out of the room.* You refuse to entertain the question: 'That is another topic. It is not what we're here to discuss', 'This is far too complex a question to deal with here', 'I'm afraid we simply don't have time to deal with that today.'

## When someone else is in the chair

When someone else – such as your teacher – is in the chair, responsibility for managing the question-and-answer session lies with them. You may be able to predict what they will do when you have finished your presentation. Some teachers like to begin the session by putting a question to the presenter; others by inviting questions 'from the floor' and starting a free-for-all discussion; yet others by putting a question to everyone else in the room. Some take the opportunity to deliver their own prepared mini-lecture. Some are concerned to demonstrate their own cleverness. They have power, and to that extent you are at their mercy. In that situation, do hold on to your sense of self. As we reminded you just now, you are a *student*, a person striving to learn. There is no shame in not knowing the answer to every question, or not being as clever as your teacher (yet).

# Respect your audience

In a question-and-answer session, you will sometimes get a question that is manifestly confused or ill thought out, or that shows the questioner has missed a point that you thought you had explained perfectly adequately. We urge you to treat the questioner and the question with respect.

You may have encountered presenters who respond to such questions with a 'put-down', with scorn or sarcasm. Such a dismissive response invariably deters others in the audience from raising a question of their own. A chill comes over the room, the energy level drops.

We suggest that you treat even a poor question as an opportunity to restate a point that you made, perhaps in simpler language. It may well be that there are others in the audience who didn't quite understand the first time and will welcome your going over it again.

Sometimes in a question-and-answer session, someone will make a contribution that isn't actually a question: it's a retelling of a point you made or a story based on their personal experience. Rather than respond with a snappy 'Yes, what's your question?', we suggest that you acknowledge their contribution. A few gentle words – 'That's interesting. Thank you' – will usually be sufficient.

# Part Eight

# Evaluation

# How did it go? What have you learned?

## Immediately after

You never know in advance how you will feel when your presentation is over and you've left the room. It's rather like taking an unseen exam: you might come out feeling exhilarated because you think you've done well, depressed because you think it's been a disaster, or simply relieved because it's over and you can get on with your life. Whichever is the case, your emotions will almost certainly be running high when you've just finished.

For that reason, straight after your presentation is not a good time to hold an 'inquest'. It is, however, a time when you may be on the receiving end of other people's comments on it. These may vary widely in tone and content: from congratulation to commiseration, from constructive support to condescension. Sometimes people say the most tactless things, even if they're trying to be

**135**

supportive. They seem to feel they're entitled to express to you their judgments on your performance. You may also encounter unspoken comment: the 'pointed silence'. Not surprisingly, given how strongly criticism is emphasized in some universities, words of appreciation often don't come spontaneously into people's mouths.

(When you have been in the audience for someone else's presentation, remember that this is a moment for positives. It would be extraordinary if you were unable to find at least one unambiguously positive thing to say about their presentation, so look for it and say it!)

How should you respond to other people's comments if you're feeling a bit vulnerable? Our advice on responding to aggressive or poor questions may be relevant here. Don't rise to provocation, or let yourself be wounded by it. (Easier said than done? Remember that a provocative statement says more about the person making it than the person receiving it.) The usual gentle words – 'That's interesting. Thank you' – will usually suit the situation.

## Reviewing your presentation

A day or two after you've given your presentation will usually be a good time to review it. Get out the prompts that you used and go through them: use them to recreate your presentation in your mind.

Now ask your review questions. First, 'What went well?' What points were you able to make successfully? What went down well – whether content or how you presented it – with your audience? Make notes on all your observations.

Next, ask 'What didn't go so well?' Where did you miss out a step in your reasoning? What howlers did you commit? (All presenters look back and cringe at things they've said or done and wish they hadn't. You're in good company!) What points did you have trouble persuading your audience to accept? Again, make notes on all your observations.

## Learning lessons

Now, with your review notes in front of you, ask yourself: 'What would I do in the same way next time? And what would I do differently?' Make a note of your answers. If you have another presentation to do shortly, you'll have your answers at the back of your mind while you are preparing it, and the improvement process will be under way automatically.

If there were one or two people in your audience whose judgment and sympathy you trust, now would be a good time to ask their advice about improving your presentation performance. When you're looking forward rather than back, it will be easier to take their comments on board and use them constructively.

Good luck!

### Web links, feedback, updates

Links to useful websites can be found by logging on to

www.student-friendly-guides.com

If you have any questions about giving a presentation that this book hasn't covered, or any suggestions for improving it, please log on to the website and email them to us. We'll be glad to answer any questions, and all suggestions for improvements will be very gratefully received.

And don't forget to check out the website regularly for updates to this and other Student-Friendly Guides, and for useful web links.

# EXCELLENT DISSERTATIONS!
Peter Levin

*"Such well thought through and clearly explained support tools are a breath of fresh air!"*
*BSc Social Policy student*

Producing a dissertation is a major requirement of an increasing number of courses. The dissertation is likely to be the largest single piece of work you will be asked to produce. *Excellent dissertations!* guides you through the whole process: planning your dissertation project, managing it, and writing it up. The book offers friendly and practical advice. It addresses all the questions students ask, including:

- How do I choose a topic?
- How should I manage my time?
- How can I make best use of my supervisor?
- How many chapters should my dissertation have?
- Which is the best referencing system to use?

*Excellent dissertations!* is a must for every student with a dissertation to do. It is a lively, concise and to-the-point guide, which will steer you through the entire process.

**Contents:** Introduction / **Part One: Preliminaries** / Formal requirements and arrangements / Pleasing the examiners / You and your supervisor / **Part Two: Getting started** / The 'twin-track': your project and your dissertation / Project and dissertation: Exploring the literature / Project: Making a shortlist of possible subjects / Project: Selecting your preferred subject / Project: Methodology / Project: Materials / Project and dissertation: Time management and planning / **Part Three: The 'middle period'** / Keeping everything under control / Project: Being your own manager / Dissertation: Creating your literature review / Dissertation: Developing your outline **/ Part Four: The 'endgame'** / The challenge to complete / Project: Concluding your work / Dissertation: Improving your draft / Dissertation: Conforming to good academic practice / Dissertation: Final editing / Notes and references / Acknowledgments.

*136pp 0 335 21822 9   (EAN  9 780335 218226)   Paperback*

# WRITE GREAT ESSAYS!

Peter Levin

*"One of my favourite books! It helped me to read quickly and efficiently and to find what I want. The bullet-pointed statements pointed me in the right direction to getting better grades."*

BA History student

*"Gives a clear picture of the requirements – I had no idea how to deal with huge amounts of material, and this guide made me more effective. It helped many of my classmates too and I recommend it to other students with no hesitation."*

MSc Social Policy student

A must for every student with an essay to write!

- How to deal with 'academic-speak' and monster reading lists
- How to choose and use an efficient reading and note-taking strategy
- How to clarify awkward essay topics
- How to find the right structure for your essay
- How to avoid accusations of plagiarism

This lively, concise, to-the-point guide will help you study and write efficiently and effectively. It offers hints and practical suggestions so you can develop good study skills and build your confidence. With this guide you can get the grades you deserve for the work you put in. No student should be without it!

**Contents:** Introduction /**Part One: Getting started** / 'I'm a slow reader' / Three stages in academic learning / Coping with monster reading lists / **Part Two: Reading purposes and strategies** / What are you reading for? / Making notes and translating 'academic-speak' / Exploratory reading: How to summarize a publication / Dedicated reading: How to make the material 'yours' / **Part Three: Targeted reading** / The principles behind targeted reading / How to identify key terms / How to scan a book / **Part Four: Writing essays** / Discovering what's wanted from you / How to clarify your topic / Thinking it through: a note on methodology / An all-purpose plan / Using quotations / The writing process / **Part Five: Referencing systems** / Using and citing sources / Which system to choose? / Recording details of your sources / **Part Six: Plagiarism and collusion** / The conscientious student's predicament / How academic learning forces you to plagiarize / Avoiding accusations of plagiarism / The politics of plagiarism.

*136pp   0 335 21577 7   (EAN  9 780335 215775)   Paperback*

# SUCCESSFUL TEAMWORK!
Peter Levin

*"This kind of advice needs to be stressed by tutors – but it isn't!"*
*MSc Economics student*

*"Indispensable. This guide made me more aware of basic ideas which I would not normally have thought about."*
*BSc Psychology student*

This lively, concise, to-the-point guide offers hints and practical suggestions to help you deal with the issues you face when working on a group project. It helps you to understand what goes on in project groups, to move forward in difficult situations, and to draw valuable lessons from the experience.

- How to share out the work
- How to transform your group into a team
- How to take decisions
- How to deal with 'free-riders'
- How to work constructively with someone you don't like
- How to make the most of your experience when applying for jobs

A must for every student working on a group project, and especially recommended if you have been put in a group, assigned a project and left alone to get on with it!

**Contents: Part One: Basics and context** / What do we mean by 'a team'? / The benefits of working in a team / Teamwork skills / Academic teamwork and the job market / **Part Two: Getting started** / Get in your groups / Get to know one another / Formulate your ground rules / The value of ground rules / Mission statements / Communication / Meetings / Taking decisions / Check out your assignment and plan your work / The project brief / The elements of project work / Programmes of work: the 'critical path'/ Allocating tasks / **Part Three: How are we doing?** / Progress on the project / Progress from 'group' to 'team'/ Personal progress / **Part Four: Perspectives on team behaviour** / Tensions: the task, the team and the individual / Team roles / Management systems and team organization / Team development: forming, storming, norming, performing ... / The decision-making process / Negotiation / Cultural traits and differences / Individual traits: 'cats' and 'dogs' / **Part Five: Teamwork issues and solutions** / The task: getting the work done / Getting help from your teachers / Sharing the work load: 'social loafing'/ The 'free rider' problem / Focusing on the task / Taking decisions: 'risky shift', 'group polarization' and 'groupthink' / Personal and inter-personal issues / The group that doesn't storm / Getting your multi-cultural group to 'bond' / Do teams need leaders? /Dealing with a team member who tries to dominate / Working constructively with someone you don't like / Finding your place in the team / **Part Six: Benefiting from the experience** / Getting feedback – including appreciation / Reflection / Learning logs / Reflective reports / Applying for jobs / Polishing up your CV / Being interviewed / Group tests in assessment centres / Notes and references / Further reading / Background and acknowledgments.

*136pp   0 335 21578 5   (EAN  9 780335 215782)   Paperback*

# SAIL THROUGH EXAMS!

Peter Levin

*"A good read. The clear explanations of how to prepare for exams and ways to choose and answer questions are practical and useful."*
BA Geography student

*"Relevant for exams and how I should approach my studies. It was easy to synthesize the information given – and comforting! My problems don't seem unique to me any more."*
MSc Management student

This lively, concise, to-the-point guide offers hints and practical suggestions to help you develop good exam-preparation skills and build your confidence, so you can get results that do justice to the work you've put in.

- How to use past exam papers
- How to decode difficult-to-understand exam questions
- How to structure top-quality answers
- How to revise effectively
- How to get in the right frame of mind for exams
- How to do your best on the day

A must for every student preparing for traditional exams!

**Contents:** Introduction / **Part One: Using past exam papers** / Get hold of past exam papers / What to look for in past exam papers / Unfair questions / The guessing game: What topics will come up this year? / **Part Two: Formulating model answers** / What are examiners looking for? / Interpreting the question / Methodology / Materials / Drawing up a plan /An alternative approach: the 'question string' / Choose your introduction / Argument or chain of reasoning? / Writing exam answers: some more suggestions / Questions for examiners / **Part Three: In the run-up to exams** / Revising effectively / Memorizing / Make best use of your time / Getting in the right frame of mind for exams / **Part Four: On the day of the exam** / Be organized / Further Reading / Acknowledgments.

*136pp   0 335 21576 9   (EAN  9 780335 215768)   Paperback*